Grassroots

and

Coalitions

Grassroots *and* Coalitions

Exploring the Possibilities of Black Politics

National Political Science Review, Volume 15

Michael Mitchell
David Covin, *editors*

A Publication of the National Conference of Black Political Scientists

Transaction Publishers
New Brunswick (U.S.A.) and London (U.K.)

Library of Congress Catalog Number: 2013011203
ISBN: 978-1-4128-5261-6
Printed in the United States of America

Library of Congress Cataloging-in-Publication Data

Grassroots and coalitions : exploring the possibilities of Black politics / Michael Mitchell and David Covin, editors.
    pages cm.
  Includes bibliographical references.
  ISBN 978-1-4128-5261-6
  1. African Americans—Politics and government—21st century. 2. State government—United States. 3. Local government—United States. 4. Political participation—United States. 5. African Americans—Relations with Hispanic Americans—Political aspects. I. Mitchell, Michael, 1944– editor of compilation. II. Covin, David, 1940– editor of compilation.
  E185.615.G6716 2013
  323.1196'073—dc23
                                           2013011203

Contents

Editors' Note

The title for this volume of the *National Political Science Review* (*NPSR*), "Grassroots and Coalitions: Exploring the Possibilities of Black Politics," stands as the organizing theme for the volume's peer-reviewed research articles. Each in its own way explores the patterns of power competition at the state and local levels in American politics.

In a country the size of a continental nation like the United States, quite clearly power is dispersed across varied types of power structures. Most frequently, the lion's share of attention goes to national level power structures and national political institutions. Nevertheless, the competition for power and the pursuit of the goals of Black politics, which encompass those of striving for social and economic equality, a strengthening of collective Black agency, and the political autonomy of Black political actors, take place across the multilayered terrain of American politics.

During and after the historic civil rights campaigns of the 1960s, Black mayors appeared as new figures of power and authority. They were placed into office by commanding insurgencies, mobilized both against the eroding hold of old incumbents, perceived as perpetrators of inequality, as well as by a sense of Black agency, articulated in Black nationalist and "Black power" terms. Pioneering mayors such as Carl Strokes of Cleveland, Richard Hatcher of Gary, Kenneth Gibson of Newark, and Harold Washington of Chicago represented changes in the power structure of American politics.

The research articles in this volume take another look at Black power emergence, but from different angles, and under the changed historical circumstances of more than forty years since the first breakthroughs. Enough time has lapsed to warrant a new look at the circumstances and terrain in which Black politics is played out at the lower reaches of American politics. These articles probe, for example, an apparent enduring capacity of Black agency to elect Black candidates at the state and local levels. They explore whether Black agency fits within the contours and limits of established political institutions and practices. One article probes the classic proposition of "racial fear" and examines the ability of Black candidates to win state-wide elections with crucial White support (Thomas Carsey and Jason Windett). Another article looks at the impact of local political organizations in enhancing the chances of Black candidates in winning local races (Mica Kubic). The other articles raise the question of whether Black agency has matured sufficiently to take on the newer challenges of Black politics: forming meaningful coalitions with minority groups similarly situated in the social, economic, and political pyramids of American society. Tatishe Nteta and Kevin Wallsten look at the messages of Black pastors regarding affinities with the Latino community, and Sharon Wright et al. investigate the extent of the differences in the participatory styles of poor Blacks and poor Whites.

In this issue we introduce a special section on the recent presidential election. We asked several members of the National Conference of Black Political Scientists (NCOBPS), our parent organization, to submit brief essays on what they regard as the more important aspects of the election. The essays highlight the enduring changes that have occurred in Black American politics marked by President Obama's election to a second term. These changes took place as Black American politics has confronted new complexities, particularly regarding measures of voter suppression, and partisan polarization directed against the Obama presidency. Despite these new obstacles, Black Americans voted in unprecedented numbers. As one of the essays (Christopher Stout and Katherine Tate) argues, the response to these challenges suggests a growing sophistication in employing counter tactics within the electoral arena itself.

Another essay (Wendy G. Smooth) underscores the presence of Black women voters in this electoral contest. Black women reached the highest voting turnout of all ethnic, racial, and gender constituencies in President Obama's re-election. They were key to Obama's success. The essay further argues that Black women are, therefore, entitled to recognition in the form of a prominent place in President Obama's second-term policy agenda.

The third essay (Charles E. Jones and Karin L. Stanford) takes on the issue of President Obama's outreach strategy to his non-White constituencies. In question is Obama's first-term efforts to soften the ways in which he articulated issues that would directly impact Blacks, Latinos, gays, and lesbians. During this campaign, however, he felt compelled to speak more forcefully and clearly to these groups. In effect, he reversed himself on his deracializing strategy. The effect of this reversal was shown concretely in the increased numbers of support that he received from these constituencies. An unambiguous appeal to these voting blocks resulted in increased support, which belied predictions that support from these groups would decline because of their disenchantments with Obama.

Our "Works in Progress" section includes interesting and maybe unexpected contributions. One of our contributors, Shelby Lewis, is an administrator who has labored long in the vineyard of creating international links among Black scholars and like communities in the world. She shows how Black political scientists can devote their efforts as much to institution building as to primarily research. Another essay takes an interesting tack in theorizing about Black politics. Melissa Nobles, whose background is in comparative politics, explains how models or theories of racial violence employed in her field can be used to look at racial violence in the United States. Ollie Johnson discusses how the subject of Black politics extends outside our borders to occurrences and patterns in Brazil. James Jennings describes his longstanding interest in the urban terrain of Black politics. His reflections highlight the importance of this aspect of Black politics. It provides further context for the thrust and underlying concerns of the research articles in this volume.

This issue's book review section provides critical assessments of several facets of Black politics. Featured in this section is an extended reflection of Manning Marable's much discussed and controversial biography of Malcolm X. The reviewer, Melanye Price, takes on the tasks of appraising Marable's work, as well as of offering a fresh perspective on the Malcolm X myth and of pointing out the need for refashioning the myth for a contemporary readership imbued with the currents of thought, such as feminism, that were underappreciated during Malcolm X's time. Reviews of two books on Black representation assess the actual power and influence that Black representatives possess in Congress. They point to the limits of Black representation on this plane and raise the important question of whether institutionalized representation indeed delivers real power and benefit for Blacks as a whole. Several other books reviewed extend the reach of the study of Black politics beyond the borders of the United States. They suggest that the questions underlying the analysis of domestic Black politics find similar resonance in other racialized societies such as South Africa.

Lastly, we publish an essay by William Strickland, in memory of Ron Walters. Walters was a stalwart supporter of both the NPSR and NCOBPS. Strickland's effort lays out the political world underlying much of Professor Walters' work. Its emphasis is on the context which grounded his inspiring contributions for Black scholars and activists alike.

Articles

The Contextual Effects of Race, Racial Representation, and Elite Campaign Cues on Voter Behavior in Statewide Races

Thomas M. Carsey
University of North Carolina
Jason Windett
Saint Louis University

Introduction

Race plays an undeniably important role in electoral politics in the United States. Scholars have paid particular attention to how White voters respond to candidates viewed as sympathetic to the interests of African Americans. Most of this work rests on Key's (1949) seminal statement about the perceived threat that southern Whites might feel in response to living in places with relatively large Black populations. Key's racial threat hypothesis (*see also* Blalock 1967) predicted that Whites would show greater support for candidates perceived as hostile to Black interests as the Black population density increased in their surrounding area. This prediction assumes that: (a) Whites have political interests that differ from Blacks, (b) Whites should be expected to reject candidates who do not represent their unique interests, and (c) larger Black populations represent a political/electoral threat to what would otherwise be White dominance of local politics. Taken together, these factors create the imperative among White voters to work against candidates who might support Black interests. Of course, Key's original idea rested on more than just perceived difference in political interests—it rested on White racism.

At a more fundamental level, the racial threat hypothesis relies on the expected response of Whites to social/political interaction and experience with Blacks. The racial threat hypothesis assumes a hostile White reaction that will continue unabated. However, Key's original work focused only on the South, and at a time when the political "threat" posed by Blacks to Whites rested on expectations rather than experience. Whites in Key's South had not experienced any consequences—positive or negative—based on actual Black political power at least since Reconstruction. Rather, Key argued that Whites feared what they *might* experience.

While Key's prediction is simple and straightforward, subsequent research has produced mixed results. While numerous explanations have been offered for these varied results, we suggest that two factors are critical in the contemporary period. First, many

3

Whites now have actual experience with Black political power in the form of living in a place that has been served by a Black elected official. Such Whites can respond based on that experience rather than just on their expectations. Second, the specific context of an individual campaign—in particular whether it has been "racialized" or not—might also affect how Whites respond to the racial make-up of the place within which they reside. Both of these factors constitute part of the larger racial context within which a given election takes place. In short, we think the existing evidence may be mixed because specific elections take place in different contexts that include different elite political rhetoric regarding the question of race. In other words, the mixed results reported in more recent studies may reflect a failure to consider contest-specific factors in a contemporary political environment where the politics of race have become more subtle and complex.

In this paper, we enter into this debate by examining the reported voting behavior of Whites when faced with a statewide election involving a Black candidate. We focus particular attention on the question of expectations versus experience and whether race was made an explicit issue during the campaign. Specifically, we model how White voters respond to the racial make-up of their surroundings as well as their personal experience with Black elected officials when casting a ballot in a statewide election involving a Black candidate. We analyze reported vote choice using survey data from five such contests that occurred in 2006. Our findings, much like others in the current literature, are mixed. However, we view such findings as evidence of the need for a more nuanced theory of the impact of racial context on voting behavior. In particular, we suggest that the impact of contextual factors previously examined in the literature likely depends on the particular ways in which race is or is not highlighted as part of an election campaign. We argue that scholars need to devote more attention to the unique events and activities of a particular election context in order to understand the role played by race.

The Role of Contextual Effects and Prior Experience

Key's (1949) original presentation of the racial threat hypothesis described the response of Whites to high levels of Black population density within an area as driven by fear.[1] This purported fear emerged from a belief that White and Black citizens would have different political interests. Thus, any political gains made by African Americans would necessarily result in political losses for Whites. These gains and losses extend beyond just votes. The real threat was to come in the resulting behavior of government and the policies produced by it if African Americans were to gain influence. While Key's work focused on the South and was supported by additional work by Wright (1977), Huckfeldt and Kohfeld (1989) demonstrated that the negative White response to the size of the Black population surrounding them was a national phenomenon and not just a southern one. Other scholars find similar support for the notion that White fear of Blacks and an underlying prejudice toward Blacks drives the voting behavior of Whites when going to the polls for city mayoral elections (Holli and Green 1989; Grimshaw 1992; Rivlin 1992). Much of this early work focused only on White candidates who might be seen as more or less sympathetic to the interests of African Americans. However, White prejudice extends to Black candidates as well, and has been seen as a critical and unwavering staple of American politics that cannot be overcome by increasing political knowledge or acceptance of Black political candidates (Bell 1992).

The racial threat hypothesis, however, is not the whole story. Some scholars report evidence of a positive response among White voters toward Black political candidates resulting either from higher Black population densities (Carsey 1995) or prior experience with a Black elected official (Hajnal 2001, 2007). These and other findings (see the debate between Giles and Buckner 1993, 1996; Voss 1996; *see also* Oliver and Mendelbert 2000) suggest a more mixed response among Whites than that predicted by the original racial threat hypothesis. We suspect that one key element that may help sort out these mixed findings centers on actual experience versus expected outcomes when faced with an electoral choice that could potentially pit Black interests against the interests of Whites. We suspect that experiencing social and political interaction with Blacks, as well as experiencing Black political power in the form of elected leaders, may temper any potentially negative reactions by Whites, and may even reverse them. This may stem from social interaction reducing feelings of prejudice and the sense of "us" versus "them" among Whites. It may also be a pragmatic realization that Whites living in places with relatively larger Black populations have shared rather than conflicting political interests with their Black neighbors. Finally, having a Black elected official who then demonstrates to Whites that their fears were not in fact realized may be what is at work. Carsey (1995) speculates more about the first two possibilities while Hajnal (2001, 2007) focuses more on the third. Regardless of the mechanism, we suspect that experience with what actually happens trumps fears of what might happen, thereby reducing or even reversing the perceived racial threat Whites may feel.

The underlying assumption of the racial threat hypothesis is the notion of Whites being afraid of significant Black political influence, represented in the extreme by the electoral success of Black candidates. Such Whites may feel a Black leader will alter the status quo and only consider policies beneficial to the Black community (Kinder and Sanders 1996). Without prior experience with Black elected officials to dispel this notion, voters rely on low information cues. In these situations, cues such as political party affiliation and incumbency status become important in deciding for whom to vote. However, race may also serve as a low information cue, at least to White voters, shaping their voting behavior as a result (Williams 1990; Terkildsen 1993; McDermott 1998). Given the uncertainty of how Black leaders might alter policy in favor of Black constituents, when race is among the cues available, White voters may respond negatively. In other words, uncertainty about the politics of the Black candidate offers incentives for Whites to vote for the perceived status quo, which is the White candidate (Kinder 1986; Jackman 1977).

Hajnal (2001, 2007) argues that Whites learn from the political behavior of Black elected officials and that this information dispels their most prejudicial fears of Black political power. Hajnal shows that incumbent Black mayors increase their support among White voters in re-election campaigns due to a lessening fear of Black leadership. We extend this work by considering whether experience with one type of Black elected official transfers to how Whites evaluate another Black candidate running for a different (and in our case, higher-level) office. If this happens, then any visible Black representation will increase the probability of Whites voting for a Black candidate for statewide office (assuming

Whites have a positive experience on an average with Black leadership), or at least it should reduce the probability of voting against them simply due to race. By learning about Black political behavior through previous experience with elected officials, the underlying prejudice or fears Whites have with Black candidates should dissipate.

To be clear, by experience we do not mean that White voters must have direct or personal interactions with an African American elected official. Rather, we simply mean that Whites living in a jurisdiction that elects a Black official can observe and evaluate whether and how policies and governance change as a result. The crux of Hajnal's and our argument is that this sort of experience helps to allay the concerns some White voters might otherwise have.

The second aspect of our theory involves the role of social interaction. Allport (1954) argues that members of different groups will feel lower levels of prejudice toward each other when a common goal is at stake. In reaching this goal, the opposing groups will interact frequently and as equals. This interaction erodes the prior prejudice and negative view that individuals held of members of the opposition group. Carsey (1995) speculates that such social interaction is responsible for his finding that increases in Black population within urban neighborhoods led White voters in those neighborhoods to be more supportive of voting for a Black mayoral candidate in New York and Chicago. The main idea is that the social context of a community works to dispel racial fears and prejudice. In these situations, the interaction of Blacks and Whites in a community environment diminishes the prejudice of Whites due to their acceptance of the lifestyles and behavior of their Black neighbors. Even if such social interaction does not reduce racial animosity, it may be that Whites living in neighborhoods with large Black populations expect such areas to benefit under Black political leadership, thus realizing that they have a shared political interest with their Black neighbors rather than a competing one—if a pothole in your neighborhood gets fixed, you may not care why.

To summarize thus far, we suspect that the mixed findings in the current literature may stem from insufficient attention given to the overall experience Whites have with Blacks living in their immediate surroundings and/or serving as their elected representatives. The potential threat can be replaced by real experience. Some Whites might interpret their experience in similarly negative terms, but others may come to view the perceived "threat" as false, and still others may conclude that they have a shared interest with Black citizens rather than interests that are opposed. Before turning to our analysis, however, two more factors merit consideration.

First, nearly all of the existing scholarly work in this area has wedded Black political interests with Democratic Party candidates. Most of these analyses do not involve actual Black candidates, but those that do are generally limited (due to historical reality) to Black candidates who are Democrats. Given the historic connection between African Americans and the Democratic party at least since the 1930s, which only strengthened in the 1960s, this linkage in the literature makes sense. This pattern means that voters were not generally cross-pressured when faced with a Black candidate, but it also means that separating support/opposition for candidates based on party versus race has been difficult. Work that has examined how Whites respond to Black candidates has principally focused on the absence/presence of the so-called Bradley effect, whereby public opinion polls prior to an election tend to overestimate a Black candidate's support relative to their performance on election day (see Hopkins 2009 for a review). In three of the five statewide races we examine that featured a Black candidate running against a White candidate, the Black candidate was a Republican. This presented voters with a signal at odds with the typical association between party and race. It is unclear how we would expect voters to respond in this circumstance. Carsey (2000) shows evidence that voters recognized four cases in 1989 when the Republican candidate for governor was decidedly more pro-choice on abortion than was the Democrat. In each case, pro-choice voters showed greater support for the pro-choice Republican while pro-life voters showed greater support for the pro-life Democrat—controlling for a host of other factors including party identification. However, in Carsey's (2000) case, abortion was a particularly salient issue in each campaign. In our three contests involving a Black Republican, the race of the candidates was no secret, but it was not a central feature of any of these campaigns.

This raises the final, and potentially most important, concern for our analysis—whether or not a particular electoral contest is explicitly framed for voters in racial terms. An ongoing debate continues in the literature regarding racial frames, racial priming, and prejudice. The early debate focused on the potential divide between direct versus symbolic racism (e.g., Kinder and Sears 1989; Sniderman et al. 1991). More recent work suggests that the contemporary political environment will not support explicit racial appeals. Explicit racial framing may actually produce sympathy rather than hostility as the social norm against explicit racism overwhelms any underlying racism that Whites might hold (e.g., Mendelberg 2001).[2]

In more general terms, scholars have argued that strategic candidates employ a variety of tactics to re-frame a campaign along terms that advantage their candidacy, trying to induce what Riker (1990) calls heresthetic change (*see also* Carsey 2000). Substantial research shows that voters respond either directly or indirectly to such strategies (e.g., Carsey 2000; Druckman et al. 2004), but Mendelberg's (2001) findings suggest that employing such a strategy around race may have mixed effects. For much of U.S. history, Black candidates for public office facing a majority-White electorate rarely ran racialized or explicitly pro-Black campaigns due to a concern about potential White backlash (Lupia and McCubbins 1998). The argument is that Black candidates themselves do not want to appeal to the underlying fear of Black leadership. More recently, this has changed somewhat (e.g., Powell 2008; Perry 2009), but it still remains the case that when race is introduced into the campaign, it is generally by the (White) candidate who seeks to prime a perceived racial division in the electorate. In bi-racial elections, White candidates represent the status quo in terms of racial politics. If White candidates feel electorally threatened by their Black opponents, they may try to change the frame of the campaign's focus to one that plays off the implicit anxiety that White voters might feel toward African Americans.

From this discussion, we frame our primary theoretical contribution as whether White voters respond to the racial make-up of their social context and/or to their experience with being represented by Black elected officials, and if so, whether those responses are positive or negative, will likely depend upon how elites frame the question of race during the campaign. Our argument is similar to that offered by Dyck and Pearson-Merkowitz (2010) in that voters' social contexts likely interact with the elite political stimuli they experience to determine how they respond to their social contexts. Thus, our primary argument is that failure to consider this conditional relationship between social context and elite behavior may also be contributing to the mixed findings we observe in the literature regarding the racial threat hypothesis. We argue that a campaign that highlights race as a meaningful political cleavage should at least increase the marginal impact of experience with other Black elected officials and/or the size of the local Black population on the voting behavior of Whites. In other words, following Carsey's (2000) more general theory regarding the conditional impact of campaigns, we expect the salience or importance of Black context and experience with Black leaders to increase for White voters when contexts involving a Black candidate become racialized by the candidates and the news media.

Data and Models

For this study, we examine survey data from White respondents living in five states holding statewide races in 2006 where one of the two major party candidates was an African American. The five states and races are Maryland (Senate), Ohio (Governor), Pennsylvania (Governor), Tennessee (Senate), and Massachusetts (Governor). The races in Maryland, Ohio, and Pennsylvania saw a Black Republican running against a White Democrat. In Tennessee and Massachusetts, voters selected between a Black Democrat and a White Republican.

The survey data come from the 2006 Cooperative Congressional Elections Study (CCES). The CCES surveyed about 38,000 respondents nationally as part of a multiteam effort. The survey itself was administered online to a sample of opt-in respondents who were chosen to be representative of the national population using a matching algorithm. If there is a bias in the CCES data, it is that it appears to over-represent individuals who are interested in politics and more likely to vote. Thus, the CCES might be better thought of as representing the attentive public or the electorate rather than the general public. Of course, the focus of this analysis is on the reported behavior of voters, so the CCES is quite appropriate. As we outline below, we also control for a number of standard predictors of vote choice that are themselves likely to absorb many of the differences in attentiveness to politics that distinguish this sample from the general public.[3] The CCES is also the only data set based on a common survey instrument that has a sufficient number of respondents from these five states to perform the analyses presented here.

Our analysis focuses on only White respondents residing in one of these five states. To these data we add measures of the racial population density of the area in which a respondent lived as well as whether they had previous experience being represented by a Black elected official in their area. We measure Black population density at the level of the five-digit U.S. Postal ZIP code. This is the smallest geographical unit available to us in the CCES survey and is designed to tap into the potential for White voters to have meaningful social interaction with African Americans. It is the closest we can come with these data to measuring "neighborhood" racial context. The specific measure comes from the 2000 U.S. Census's report of the proportion of residents in a ZIP code who reported being Black or African American. Our measure ranges from 0 to .96, with a mean of 0.094 and a standard deviation of 0.171.[4]

Our measure of prior experience with being represented by a Black elected official is recorded as a simple dummy variable, coded "1" for such prior experience and "0" otherwise. We measured experience as living in a place that was currently or had previously been represented in the U.S. House of Representatives by an African American or living in a city of more than 50,000 residents that has had an African American mayor.[5] Again, our experience measure merely records whether a respondent currently lives in a place that is currently or has recently been represented by a Black elected official. It does not capture anything about the actual interaction respondents may have had with their representative, nor does it measure how respondents felt about having a Black representative.[6] The question is whether the simple fact of living in a jurisdiction with a history of having had a Black representative in the U.S. House or as mayor, translates into how White voters respond to the opportunity to vote for an African American candidate for a state-wide office. The list of African American representatives and mayors was compiled from the Joint Center for Political and Economic Studies and the Office of the Clerk of the United States House of Representatives. About 19 percent of the White respondents identified in our data lived in a place with a history of being represented by an African American House member and/or mayor. The dependent variable in each analysis is the vote choice reported by the individual White respondent in the survey. To test our theory, this variable is coded "1" if the respondent reported voting for the Black candidate and "0" if the respondent reported voting for the White candidate.

Our models also include a number of control variables. First, we control for the effect of partisanship using two dummy variables. The first is coded "1" if the respondent is of the same political party identification as the Black candidate and "0" otherwise. The second partisan dummy variable is coded "1" if the respondent is from the opposing political party and "0" otherwise. The result is nonparty identifiers being the baseline referent group. We include a control variable for gender, coded "1" for females and "0" for males. Categorical measures of individual-level education and income are also included in our models. Due to the partisanship of the candidates, we coded the income and education variables to move in the same expected direction based on expected vote choice. For education, the variable is coded 1–6, moving from low education to high education for the Black Democratic candidates, while the variable moves from high education to low education for Black Republican candidates. We use the same approach for income, a fifteen-category variable. For Black Democratic candidates, the income variable ranges from poor to rich values, while for Black Republican candidates, the order is reversed. Finally, we include the median income of the ZIP code in thousands of dollars to ensure that any effect of racial density we uncover is not an artifact of contextual differences in income instead. This variable ranges from just under $11,000 up to about $140,000.

We contend that the specific circumstances surrounding an electoral contest likely condition the impact of racial context on the behavior of White voters when faced with a Black candidate. The list of such factors certainly includes whether the context was racialized by one or more of the candidates involved, whether the Black candidate was a Democrat or a Republican, the history of racial politics in the state, the spending and/or campaign advertising of the candidates, and the visibility of the Black candidates involved in the race, just to name a few. With only five contests to consider, we simply cannot pool our data and include contest-level measures of these factors. The best alternative is to estimate our vote-choice models separately for each of these five contests and then draw comparisons between them.[7] With that in mind, we provide a brief review of each contest before turning to our quantitative analysis.[8]

In the Maryland Senate race, the Black candidate, Michael Steele, was running for the open seat left vacant by the retiring Democrat Paul Sarbanes. Steele was the incumbent Republican Lieutenant Governor at the time of the election and was known as an ideological conservative. He was opposed by Benjamin Cardin, a Democratic U.S. Representative from Baltimore County. Cardin would eventually win the election with 55 percent of the vote to Michael Steele's 44 percent. Steele received about 50 percent of the White vote.

The Ohio gubernatorial race featured the incumbent Secretary of State Ken Blackwell running against U.S. Representative Ted Strickland. Blackwell, a Black Republican candidate, was seeking to retain the governorship for the Republican Party after Bob Taft was forced out of office due to term limits. Strickland, however, won this election with nearly 61 percent of the vote to Blackwell's 36 percent. Blackwell received about 40 percent of the White vote.

The Pennsylvania gubernatorial election was the only race that featured an incumbent seeking re-election. Incumbent Democratic Governor Ed Rendell was seeking to retain the office. Lynn Swann, a former professional football player for the Pittsburgh Steelers and an African American, was his Republican opponent. Swann had not previously held any elected office and ran unopposed in the Republican primary. Rendell won re-election with 60 percent of the vote to Swann's 40 percent. Swann received about 43 percent of the White vote.

The Tennessee Senate race was the most competitive of the five races included in this analysis. Tennessee's Senate seat was open after Republican Bill Frist announced his retirement after two terms. The Republican nominee, Bob Corker, was a former U.S. Senate candidate and Mayor of Chattanooga. The Democratic candidate was Harold Ford, Jr., a Black U.S. House member from Memphis. Ford is from a prominent Black political family in Tennessee. His father was a U.S. Representative and his uncle served in the Tennessee State Senate. This seat was targeted by the National Democratic Party as a potential seat gain from the Republicans. Despite the party's efforts, Corker won the election with a margin of about two percentage points. Ford received about 40 percent of the White vote. As we will discuss in more detail below, this contest was the only one of the five that was explicitly racialized as part of the campaign.

The only contest, among the five we examine, that saw a victory for the Black candidate was the Massachusetts gubernatorial election. The Massachusetts governorship was open after Republican incumbent Mitt Romney declined to seek re-election. In the ensuing election, Deval Patrick, a Black Democratic candidate, defeated Republican Lieutenant Governor Kerry Healy 56 percent to 36 percent. Patrick, a former U.S. Assistant Attorney General, became only the second Black governor in U.S. history. Patrick received about 51 percent of the White vote.

As a set, these five contests display a good deal of variation. We have races for the Senate and races for governor. We have one race including an incumbent, while the others were open-seat races. Four of the five races featured African American candidates with previous political experience. Only one of the African American candidates won, but all of them received a reasonable share of the overall vote as well as significant support from White voters. Two of the African American candidates were Democrats while the other three were Republicans. Finally, the race of the candidates was a salient issue in only one of the contests.

Analysis and Results

Table 1 presents the results of five separate logistic regression models for White voters by state of residence. The table reports coefficient estimates, their standard errors, and the change in the predicted probability of voting for the Black candidate for a one-standard deviation increase in an independent variable or, for dummy variables, moving from 0 to 1 on that dummy. For each predicted probability calculation, the other variables in the model were held at their means or, for dummy variables, at zero.

Looking at our primary explanatory variables of interest—experience with representation by a Black elected official and percent Black in the respondents ZIP code—no discernible pattern emerges across the five races. The marginal effect of representation by a Black official is only statistically significant in the case of Tennessee's Senate election. In this case, prior representation increased the predicted probability of voting for the Black candidate, Harold Ford, Jr., by about 47 percentage points. In three of the other states, the coefficient operating on the prior representation variable does not even approach traditional levels of statistical significance. Finally, the variable was dropped from the analysis in Massachusetts because all respondents with prior Black representation reported voting for the Black candidate. This does suggest a fairly strong positive effect in this particular race, but this lack of variance prevents estimating the coefficient.

The results for Tennessee merit closer attention, as they may have less to do with general prior Black representation and more to do with who the Black representative was. Harold Ford, Jr., the Black Democrat running for this Senate seat, was himself one of the prior Black representatives for some respondents in the state. The other Black elected official in Tennessee at the time was the mayor of Memphis, which happens to correspond directly to the congressional district Ford represented. Thus, our findings for Tennessee may not indicate a reversal of the racial threat hypothesis in response to experience with Black political leadership in general, but rather support for a representative who served this particular part of the state for a decade.

Interestingly, the Tennessee Senate race was also the only campaign in our study that experienced a campaign with an explicit racial tone. The Republican Party ran attack ads against Ford playing directly to the racial stereotypes held by White voters. That did not appear to hurt Ford among White voters from the Memphis area. In fact, the positive effect of the prior representation variable is consistent with a conclusion that the overtly racial strategy backfired, at least in this part of the state. We think the personal experience with Ford rather than this backfiring hypothesis is more likely, but the finding is consistent with both interpretations.

Turning next to the impact of Black population density, we again find a mixed bag of effects. In four of five states, the coefficient estimate is negative, which is consistent with the racial threat hypothesis. However, that negative coefficient only reaches traditional levels of statistical significance in two races—Ohio and Pennsylvania—while only beginning to approach it in a third—Tennessee. Given that the correlation between prior representation and the percentage Black of the population in Tennessee is 0.59, and the

Table 1.
Logit Models Predicting the Probability of Whites Voting for Black Candidate in Five Statewide Contests in 2006[a]

Variable	Maryland Coef	Pred Prob	Ohio Coef	Pred	Pennsylvania Coef	Pred Prob	Tennessee Coef	Pred	Massachusetts Coef	Pred Prob
Prior Rep.	0.239	0.05	-0.124	-0.03	0.142	0.04	2.221	0.47		
	(0.549)		(0.194)		(0.444)		(0.771)			
%Black in Zip code	-0.413	-0.05	-3.051	-0.07	-2.559	-0.07	-1.746	-0.06	3.675	0.05
	(1.081)		(0.863)		(1.413)		(1.333)		(3.793)	
Shared Partisan	3.022	0.58	2.533	0.55	1.824	0.42	2.687	0.58	3.508	0.55
	(0.417)		(0.171)		(0.158)		(0.497)		(0.739)	
Opposed Partisan	-1.844	-0.42	-3.174	-0.58	-2.242	-0.46	-3.647	-0.66	-3.013	-0.62
	(0.392)		(0.375)		(0.264)		(0.508)		(0.628)	
Income	0.058	0.06	0.009	0.01	0.026	0.03	-0.015	-0.01	-0.042	-0.03
	(0.039)		(0.020)		(0.022)		(0.042)		(0.049)	
Education	0.035	0.01	0.102	0.03	0.141	0.05	0.058	0.02	0.168	0.06
	(0.124)		(0.062)		(0.068)		(0.121)		(0.117)	
Female	0.195	0.05	-0.466	-0.10	-0.466	-0.11	0.603	0.15	-0.212	-0.05
	(0.325)		(0.162)		(0.177)		(0.321)		(0.321)	
Zip Income	-0.006	-0.02	-0.003	-0.01	-0.007	-0.02	-0.002	-0.01	-0.007	-0.03
	(0.010)		(0.007)		(0.007)		(0.011)		(0.011)	
Constant	-0.572		-0.174		-0.042		-0.598		0.650	
	(1.034)		(-1.739)		(0.527)		(0.769)		(0.867)	
Psuedo R-Squared	0.443		0.449		0.356		0.479		0.382	
Log Likelihood	-126.32		-495.82		-426.80		-139.26		-117.99	
Total Observations	332		1,357		961		387		280	

Standard Errors reported in parentheses

[a] The predicted probabilities reported in both Table 1 for continuous variables are calculated based on moving 1 standard deviation while holding dummy variables at 0 and continuous variables at their mean. The predicted probabilities for dummy variables are calculated based on moving from 0 to 1 while holding dummy variable at 0 and continuous variable at their mean.

importance of the prior representation variable in Tennessee, the standard error for our percent Black measure in Tennessee may be somewhat inflated. Across these three states, the substantive impact of an increase in the percentage of the population in a ZIP code that is Black of one standard deviation leads to a decrease in the predicted probability of Whites voting for the Black candidate of between 6 and 7 percentage points. This does not appear to be a particularly large substantive effect, but a shift in White voter behavior of 6 to 7 percentage points would have been decisive in Tennessee and would have certainly tightened the races noticeably in Ohio and Pennsylvania.

However, we are still left without a clear consistent pattern in our results, as the effect of the percent Black in a context only achieved or approached statistical significance in just three of our five elections. The two where the effect was estimated most crisply—Ohio and Pennsylvania—involved a Black Republican candidate, but the third race with a Black Republican running—Maryland—demonstrated no effect. Among the two races with a Black Democratic candidate, the effect approached statistical significance in Tennessee, where race was an explicit element of the campaign, but was indistinguishable from zero in Massachusetts.[9]

Of course, we have already reported that the Tennessee race was the only one of this group that was racialized. In this racialized context, we found evidence of a negative impact of Black racial density, but a positive impact of prior experience with a Black representative. Thus, making race a salient part of the campaign appears to have had potentially counterbalancing effects—a positive one among Whites with experience being represented by a Black elected official, but, controlling for that, a negative effect among Whites living in increasingly Black areas. We do not want to overstate findings based on a single election, but these results are at least suggestive that the impact of these two contextual variables may in fact depend on how political elites frame the issue of race for voters in a given place and time. This is consistent with our expectation that campaign-specific factors are likely to influence the degree to which White voters respond to their racial context.

As for the rest of Table 1, the explanatory variables that show the greatest impact in terms of predicting reported vote choice are the two variables measuring partisan affiliation. Of course, this is no surprise. Across all five states, individuals with the same party identification as the Black candidate had a higher predicted probability of voting for the Black candidate than did voters who do not identify with a party. Maryland and Tennessee show the greatest impact of shared partisanship, as the probability of voting for the Black candidate increased by 58 percentage points. Ohio and Massachusetts exhibit similar effects of shared partisanship as the increase in probability of voting for the Black candidate increased 55 percentage points. Shared partisanship with the Black candidate had the least impact in Pennsylvania, as shared partisans increased their probability of voting for the Black candidate by 42 percentage points. Opposed partisanship caused steep declines in the probability of voting for the Black candidate. Partisans opposite of the party of the Black candidate in Maryland and Pennsylvania reduced their probability of voting for the Black candidate by 42 and 46 percentage points, respectively, while those in Ohio, Tennessee, and Massachusetts saw declines between 58 and 68 percentage points. Clearly, even in the contest where race was highlighted, party identification is the single most important predictor of reported vote choice for White respondents.

Most of the coefficient estimates operating on the remaining control variables included in the model do not reach traditional levels of statistical significance. Gender is a significant predictor of White voter choice in Ohio, Pennsylvania, and Tennessee. In Ohio and Pennsylvania, there was a decline in the probability of women voting for the Black Republican candidate by 10 and 11 percentage points, respectively, while women in Tennessee increased their probability of voting for the Black Democratic candidate by 15 percentage points. We suspect that this pattern has more to do with the partisanship of the candidates than their race, however.

Conclusions

What can we make of our findings? Our first and most obvious conclusion is that the mixed results in the existing literature regarding the racial threat hypothesis remain mixed. We do not find a simple consistent pattern across these five elections regarding the impact of racial context on the voting behavior of Whites. Previous experience with a Black elected official was found to be statistically and substantively important only in Tennessee. However, we cannot fully untangle whether this is a general response to Black representation or is driven by experience with the particular Black candidate running that year for the Senate. In addition, the pattern of results in Tennessee is also likely shaped by the racialized nature of that particular contest. We found a bit more support for the negative racial threat hypothesis than we did for the positive social interaction hypothesis based on our measure of racial density. That effect reached or approached statistical significance in three of five races, and the effect was negative in each case. The strongest negative effects were in upper Midwest industrial states, confirming again that a negative response among Whites to increasing Black populations is not confined to either the historical or contemporary South.

The results from Tennessee are particularly instructive. In the one contest where race was highlighted as part of the campaign, we saw White voters who had been represented by a Black elected official respond positively to that experience. At the same time, we found Whites responding negatively based on the size of the Black community in their neighborhood. The latter finding is consistent with Key's racial threat hypothesis, but the former suggests a potential avenue for overcoming that threat response. The activation of race as a salient issue during a campaign may generate a negative response among White voters who have not been represented by a Black elected official, but for those who have had a Black representative, raising the issue of race during the campaign may help rather than hurt a Black candidate. Of course, all of these races took place before the election of the United States' first African American president. How race and the racial context within which voters find themselves have been affected by the experience of having a Black president remains to be seen.

While we do not come away from this study with a simple explanation of how White voters respond to Black populations or politicians, we do not conclude from this that the impact of race on U.S. electoral politics has somehow become minimal or unimportant. Rather, we suspect that the increasingly complex role of race in electoral politics defies simple explanation. Baybeck (2006) argues that the examination of the impact of racial context on Whites' behavior should extend to the consideration of multiple contexts which may potentially interact. We concur, and that perspective shaped our approach in this study as we considered three different aspects of racial context: (1) the demographic make-up of a place, (2) prior representation by Black officials, and (3) the racial tone of a particular campaign. From this perspective, the mixed findings we uncover are really to be expected. The politics of race in the United States is much more subtle and complex now than in previous years. A simple racial threat hypothesis made sense as an explanation for White voter behavior in Key's time, and was certainly applicable to the 1968 Wallace campaign studied by Wright (1977). However, in an era where African Americans have won a wide range of elective offices, where the policy issues associated with race have evolved, and where the social norms surrounding race relations have changed in many ways, we should not expect a simple model to hold across contexts.

Of course, our study still faces several limitations. We feel it is important to acknowledge these limitations and these limitations should provide some direction for future research. For example, we lack direct measures of such contextual factors as direct social interaction, more detailed campaign behavior, and media coverage. We also lack survey data over time that would permit analyzing these processes as they unfold over the course of a campaign. Like every observational cross-sectional study of social context, we also cannot control for the fact that at least some individuals self-select into the context in which they reside. We also lack direct attitudinal measures that might allow us to tap into the racial stereotypes Whites might hold regarding Blacks. Finally, we only had five races to examine. Still, this paper provides some important insights into the conditional impact of racial context on the behavior of voters.

The fundamental conclusion we have drawn from this paper is that the particular context within which an electoral contest takes place can have a major impact on whether and how race and racial issues shape how voters respond. Thus, the final take-away point we offer is the clear need for a more subtle theory of racial contextual effects and the collection of the data necessary to adequately test such a theory. We suggest that such a theory should explore the potential conditional effects resulting from the interaction between demographic and representational contextual factors and elite-level political rhetoric and other campaign-specific contextual factors designed to heighten or dampen the political salience of race in a given place and time. Contrary to many popular commentators, we do not believe that recent political events such as the election of Barack Obama, or recent trends in research that have produced mixed results, suggest that we live in a post-racialized society. Rather, we think that the role of race in society, and particularly its political relevance, remains fundamentally important. What has changed is how race matters—a process that is more complex now than in earlier eras. From a scholarly standpoint, this makes continued research in this area not only more challenging but also more interesting.

Notes

1. By no means do we imply that a "racial threat" could only be felt by Whites in response to the presence of Blacks. Walton (1997) forcefully makes the claim that African Americans may themselves feel a racial threat from conservative Whites. This study focuses on White voters because their response to Black candidates remains an open question and because, like so many other studies, our data simply lack a sufficient sample of other racial and/or ethnic groups. Clearly such data need to be collected.

2. Whether Mendelberg's finding continues to hold following the election of Barack Obama and the reactions that has provoked is not yet known. Of course, the races analyzed in this paper preceded these events, but it remains an open and important question.

3. The 2006 CCES was supported by thirty-nine universities. A total of 38,443 respondents participated in the survey. Subjects for the larger study were selected from an opt-in Internet panel based on a propensity matching technique developed by Douglas Rivers and implemented by Polimetrix and YouGov. The CCES matching algorithm was designed to mirror the national voting age population in the United States. Details of the study methodology can be found at http://icpsr.umich.edu/icpsrweb/ICPSR/studies/30141 (accessed and verified on 03/06/2013).
4. We enter the proportion of residents in a ZIP code who are Black as a standard linear predictor. This is consistent with the vast majority of the literature on the racial threat hypothesis. One thing future scholars may wish to consider is possible nonlinear relationships that might result from there being a "tipping point" or threshold effect of racial density on White voter behavior.
5. Data are not available for cities with populations of less than 50,000 residents.
6. Our measure is static and cross-sectional because that matches our survey data. Future work may want to explore how support for Black candidates evolves over time as experience with a Black representative changes over time.
7. From a methodological standpoint, the mixed findings we report below also make it clear that pooling data from these five contests together and estimating a single common statistical model would be inappropriate.
8. A more detailed discussion of each specific campaign is beyond the scope of this paper.
9. As a check, we explored whether there were any evidence of multicollinearity or a conditional relationship between the Black proportion variable and the average income of the ZIP code. The analysis revealed low negative correlations, ranging from −.22 to −.39, and no pattern of any conditional relationship.

References

Allport, Gordon W. 1954. *The Nature of Prejudice*. Cambridge, MA: Addison-Wesley.

Baybeck, Brady. 2006. "Sorting Out the Competing Effects of Racial Context." *Journal of Politics* 68: 386–96.

Bell, Derrick. 1992. *Faces at the Bottom of the Well: The Permanence of Racism*. New York: Basic Books.

Blalock, H.M. Jr. 1967. *Toward a Theory of Minority-Group Relations*. New York: Capricorn Books.

Carsey, Thomas. 1995. "The Contextual Effects of Race on White Voter Behavior: The 1989 New York City Mayoral Election." *Journal of Politics* 57: 221–28.

Carsey, Thomas. 2000. *Campaign Dynamics: The Race for Governor*. Ann Arbor, MI: University of Michigan Press.

Druckman, James, N., Lawrence R. Jacobs, and Eric Ostermeier. 2004. "Candidate Strategies to Prime Issues and Image." *Journal of Politics* 66: 1180–202.

Dyck, Joshua J., and Shanna Pearson-Merkowitz. 2010. "Welcome to the Neighborhood, Says Who? Elite Cue Giving and Majority-Minority Group Interactions." Paper presented at the Annual State Politics and Policy Conference, Springfield, Illinois, June 2–5.

Giles, Michael and Melanie Buckner. 1993. "David Duke and Black Threat: An Old Hypothesis Revisited." *Journal of Politics* 55: 702–13.

———. 1996. "Beyond Racial Threat: Failure of an Old Hypothesis in the New South: Comment." *Journal of Politics* 58: 1171–180.

Grimshaw, William. 1992. *Bitter Fruit: Black Politics and the Chicago Machine: 1931–1999*. Chicago, IL: University of Chicago Press.

Hajnal, Zoltan. 2001. "White Residents, Black Incumbents, and Declining Racial Divide." *American Political Science Review* 95: 603–17.

———. 2007. *Changing White Attitudes toward Black Political Leadership*. Cambridge: Cambridge University Press.

Holli, Melvin, and Paul Green. 1989. *Bashing Chicago Traditions, Harold Washington's Last Campaign*. Grand Rapids, MI: William Eerdmans Publishing.

Hopkins, Daniel. 2009. "No More Wilder Effect, Never a Whitman Effect: Why and When Polls Mislead about Black and Female Candidates." *Journal of Politics* 71: 769–81.

Huckfeldt, Robert, and Carol Kohfeld. 1989. *Race and the Decline of Class in American Politics*. Urbana, IL: University of Illinois Press.

Jackman, Mary. 1977. "Prejudice, Tolerance, and Attitudes toward Ethnic Groups." *Social Science Research* 6: 145–69.

Key, V. O. 1949. *Southern Politics in State and Nation*. New York: Knopf.

Kinder, Donald. 1986. "The Continuing American Dilemma: White Resistance to Racial Change 40 Years after Myrdal." *Journal of Social Issues* 42: 151–71.

Kinder, Donald, and David Sears. 1981. "Prejudice and Politics: Symbolic Racism versus Racial Threats to the Good Life." *Journal of Personality and Social Psychology* 40: 414–31.

Kinder, Donald, and Lynn Sanders. 1996. *Divided by Color: Racial Politics and Democratic Ideals*. Chicago, IL: University of Chicago Press.

Lupia, Arthur and Matthew McCubbins. 1998. *The Democratic Dilemma: Can Citizens Learn What They Need to Know?* Cambridge: Cambridge University Press.

McDermott, Monika. 1998. "Race and Gender Cues in Low-Information Elections." *Political Research Quarterly* 51: 895–918.

Mendelberg, Tali. 2001. *The Race Card: Campaign Strategy, Implicit Messages, and the Norm of Equality*. Princeton, NJ: Princeton University Press.

Oliver, J. Eric, and Tali Mendelberg. 2000. "Reconsidering the Environmental Determinants of White Racial Attitudes." *American Journal of Political Science* 44: 574–89.

Perry, Ravi. 2009. "Black Mayors in Non-Majority Black (Medium-Sized) Cities: Universalizing the Interests of Blacks." *Ethnic Studies Review* 32: 89–130.

Powell, John. 2008. "Race, Place, and Opportunity." *The American Prospect*. September 21.

Riker, William. 1990. "Heresthetic and Rhetoric in the Spatial Model." In *Advances in the Spatial Theory of Voting*, ed. James Enelow and Melvin Hinich, 46–65. Cambridge: Cambridge University Press.

Rivlin, Gary. 1992. *Fire on the Prairie: Chicago's Harold Washington and the Politics of Race*. New York: Henry Holt.

Sniderman, Paul, M., Thomas Piazza, Philip E. Tetlock, and Ann Kendrick. 1991. "The New Racism." *American Journal of Political Science* 35: 423–47.

Terkildsen, Nayda. 1993. "When White Voters Evaluate Black Candidates: The Processing Implications of Candidate Skin Color, Prejudice, and Self-Monitoring." *American Journal of Political Science* 37: 1032–53.

Voss, D. Stephen. 1996. "Beyond Racial Threat: Failure of an Old Hypothesis in the New South." *Journal of Politics* 58: 1156–70.

Walton, Hanes Jr. 1997. *African American Power and Politics*. New York: Columbia University Press.

Williams, Linda. 1990. "White/Black Perceptions of the Electability of Black Political Candidates." *National Political Science Review* 2: 45–64.

Wright, Gerald. 1977. "Contextual Models of Electoral Behavior: The Southern Wallace Vote." *American Political Science Review* 71: 497–508.

Are Separate Struggles Really One? African American Clergy, Elite Messages, and African American Perceptions of Commonality with Latinos[*]

Tatishe Nteta
University of Massachusetts-Amherst
Kevin Wallsten
California State University-Long Beach

Simmering conflicts between Blacks and Latinos over jobs, housing, political power, and educational opportunities have attracted scholarly and popular attention for years (McClain and Karnig 1990; Meier and Stewart 1991; Meier et al. 2004; Vaca 2004). In 2003, a new chapter in the decades old story of Black-Brown relations began when the census reported, for the first time in history, that there were more Latinos than African Americans living in the United States.[1] Unsurprisingly, the announcement that Blacks were no longer the largest minority group in the United States has prompted African American and Latino leaders from across the country to publicly discuss the complexities of the relationship between their two communities. What is somewhat more surprising, however, is the uniformly positive and conciliatory tone that Black church leaders have used to characterize the interactions between Latinos and African Americans. The Reverend Al Sharpton, for example, recently claimed that, "We are not each other's enemies. We're not even each other's friends. We are the same family. We may speak a different language, have a different skin texture, but we are in the same house. And if the house burns down we are all going to die together" (Herrera 1). Echoing these sentiments, the Reverend Jesse Jackson, has said, "Indeed the current circumstances and history of African Americans and Latinos, immigrant and non-immigrant, are indelibly linked. . . . They share a history of making a way where there was no way, creating community in often hostile environments, and fighting to carve out a better future for their children." (Jackson A1). As Table 1 further illustrates, it is not difficult to find other examples of prominent African American religious leaders (those who lead particular congregations, hold denominational leadership positions, and/or have used their position to participate in electoral politics) using the pulpit to emphasize the similarities between Latinos and African Americans.[2]

The Black clergy's rhetorical emphasis on shared socioeconomic and political characteristics is by no means a recent development. Since the dawn of the civil rights movement in the 1960s, African American religious elites have drawn frequent comparisons

Table 1.
African American Religious Elites on Commonality with Latinos

Reverend Phil Lawson, Oakland, CA.	"Most African-Americans, either they or their parents migrated (to the Bay Area) from other places in the state or from the South, or Texas, looking for work, looking to better their lives, which is exactly why (Latino) immigrants migrate. There's a powerful connection between (Latino) immigrants coming into the United States and the African-American community." (O'Brien 1)
Bishop Vashti Murphy McKenzie, African Methodist Episcopal Church	"We who are Americans of African descent understand what it means to have our families separated because of politics and policies. Our ancestors of African descent saw husbands and wives separated and children sold to other locations. We understand what it means to be forced into marginalized jobs and less than minimum wage jobs. We understand what it means to be victimized by systems that depended upon our weaknesses and then profit by our strengths." (NHCLC, 1)
Reverend Joseph Lowery	"There are many differences between our experience and that of immigrant Latinos, but there is a family resemblance between Jim Crow and what is being experienced by (Latino) immigrants. Both met economic oppression. Both met racial and ethnic hostility. But the most important thing to remember is that, though we may have come over on different ships, we're all in the same damn boat now." (Lovato, 1)
Revered James Orange	"There are those who would like to separate and divide African American from brown—Latinos from African-Americans. We will not let that happen. . . . We know what it is like to be a stranger in a strange land." (Poole, 1F)
Stacy Spencer, pastor for New Direction Christian Church, Memphis, TN	"We have more in common than different. We're minority groups trying to make it in America." (Melvin, 1)
Reverend Nelson Johnson, Greensboro, NC	"I believe the question of African American-brown unity is perhaps one of the most important questions that face our nation. We are both oppressed races." (Regester, 1A)
Derrick Harkins, Senior Pastor of the Nineteenth Street Baptist Church	"We have come together to dispel the ugly myths about a African American and brown divide. . . . Throughout our history, immigrants (Latinos) have strengthened our country with their hard work and commitment to core American values. Immigrants (Latinos) are not taking our jobs or public resources. The reality is that we are unified across ethnic and racial lines." (Riley 1).

between the circumstances faced by Blacks and Latinos in the hopes of quelling potential conflicts between the two groups. Most famously, in a 1967 letter to Cesar Chavez, the Reverend Martin Luther King Jr. said of the relationship between African Americans and Latinos, "Our separate struggles are really one—a struggle for freedom, for dignity, and for humanity." (Jones and Engel 106).

The frequency and congenial nature of the intergroup messages being communicated by African American religious leaders raises an important question: do the pronouncements of religious leaders influence African American perceptions of commonality with Latinos? Unfortunately, little research has explored the extent to which elite messages are picked up by Blacks in the general public. Indeed, while a number of studies have addressed the individual and contextual determinants of African American attitudes toward Latinos (Jackson et al. 1994; Cummings and Lambert 1997; Thornton and Mizuno 1999; Oliver and Wong 2003; Gay 2006), there has been little attention paid to perceptions of commonality or the role that cues provided by African American religious elites may play in structuring these perceptions. The dearth of research assessing the impact that religious leaders have on Black perceptions of commonality is particularly surprising given the dominance of so-called "elite opinion" theory in the literature on public opinion (Lee 2002), studies which show that African Americans are markedly more religious than other racial groups (Sahgal and Smith 2009), and the extensive literature on the role of the African American church in shaping African American political behavior (McAdam 1982; Morris 1984; Walton 1985; Dawson, Brown, Allen 1990; Reese and Brown 1995; Calhoun-Brown 1996; and Harris 1999).[3]

In this article, we utilize data provided by the 2004 National Politics Study (NPS) to provide an empirical assessment of the impact that messages from religious elites may have on perceptions of political and socioeconomic commonality. Testing propositions from elite opinion theory, we find evidence that sermons, lectures, and discussions held in places of worships influence the ways African Americans think about their community's relationship with Latinos. More specifically, we show that African Americans who reported hearing a message in church on improving race relations were more likely to perceive higher levels of commonality with Latinos, to view Latinos as victims of racial discrimination, and to support building political coalitions with Latinos. Taken together, we believe these findings make a case for further explorations of the role that religious elites may play in structuring the attitudinal foundations undergirding African Americans' perceptions of commonality with Latinos.

African American Racial Attitudes

Do African Americans express feelings of commonality with Latinos? The literature on African American racial attitudes toward Latinos provides a starting point in answering this question (Jackson et al. 1994; Niemann et al. 1994; Cummings and Lambert 1997; Niemann 1999; Thornton and Mizuno 1999; Mindiola, Niemann, and Rodriguez 2002; Kaufmann 2003; Oliver and Wong 2003; Gay 2006; McClain et al. 2007). This nascent literature has reached three broad conclusions. First, African Americans do express stereotypical views of Latinos, but do so with less intensity than native Whites (Niemann et al. 1994; Cummings and Lambert 1997; Niemann 1999; Mindiola et al. 2002). Second, variables used to account for White racial attitudes toward African Americans, such as proximity (Oliver and Wong 2003; Gay 2006) and socioeconomic status (Jackson et al. 1994; Thornton and Mizuno 1995; Cummings and Lambert 1997), also help predict African American views of Latinos. Finally, Black attitudes toward Latinos are significantly influenced by levels of religiosity (Thornton and Mizuno 1995), perceptions of negative views of African Americans (Cummings and Lambert 1997), feelings of linked fate (McClain et al. 2007), and assessments of economic self-interest (Thornton and Mizuno 1999; McClain et al. 2007).

Despite the insights these studies provide into the attitudes that African Americans hold about Latinos, the literature has been plagued by a number of key problems that we believe unnecessarily limit our understanding of intergroup relations. First, the bulk of these studies employ survey data derived from the 1990s and thus do not present a contemporary view of African Americans' attitudes toward Latinos in a period in which Latinos are increasingly clashing with African Americans for scarce sociopolitical resources and power in urban America. Second, many of these studies narrowly focus their attention upon a single city rather than the nation as a whole, which elicits concerns about the generalizability of these findings (Oliver and Wong 2003; Gay 2006; McClain et al. 2007). Third, this literature tells us unfortunately little about Black perceptions of commonality with Latinos. To be more precise, existing studies of African American racial attitudes toward Latinos typically fail to examine the extent to which African Americans perceive commonality with Latinos which we define as the perception of: (1) socioeconomic similarities between the two communities; (2) similar experiences with racial discrimination and prejudice between the two communities; and (3) shared political goals, constraints, and opportunities of the two communities which make their interests inextricably bound. This lack of attention to African American perceptions of commonality is perplexing given that such perceptions are typically assigned a prominent place in theories about the construction of sustainable and successful multiracial coalitions (Browning, Marshall, and Tabb 1984; Giles and Evans 1985; Sonenshein 1990, 2003). Finally, and most importantly, many of these studies focus solely on individual-level factors in accounting for African American views of Latinos and, in doing so, fail to recognize the potential impact that contextual dynamics may have on African Americans' views of their relationship with Latinos. In particular, these studies do not address the role that social, political, and religious leaders may play in fostering or undermining strong intergroup ties.

Elite Messaging and Public Opinion

The lack of attention paid to the impact of elite messages on African American racial attitudes toward Latinos is surprising given the vaunted position that elite opinion theory has achieved in the study of public opinion. There is a long-standing consensus in political science research that information, ideas, and issue frames follow a one-way path from political elites and mainstream media to the mass public. Beginning with the early work of Berelson, Lazasfeld, and McPhee (1954) and Downs (1957), numerous scholars have hypothesized that the "rational ignorance" of ordinary citizens leads them to pay little attention to political affairs and to rely instead on cues from political elites when forming their political judgments. As suggested above, this approach to studying the dynamics of attitude formation and change, which implies that public opinion is essentially top-down and elite-driven, has come to dominate the contemporary literature on public opinion.[4]

Elite opinion theory has typically been used to explain attitudinal shifts on remote and complex issues (where there are good *a priori* reasons to expect that elites matter). There is, however, a significant body of work into elite opinion leadership on the comparatively "easy" issue of race relations. Carmines and Stimson (1989), Zaller (1992), and Lee (2002), for instance, all argue that the change in racial attitudes toward African Americans and the corresponding support for federal policies aimed at providing equal rights for African Americans were the result of changes in rhetoric among elite actors in the middle part of the twentieth century. Similarly, scholars examining the role of racial priming have demonstrated that subtle cues reflecting stereotypical attitudes concerning

African Americans offered by elites in campaigns have influenced policy preferences as well as candidate evaluations and preferences (Mendelberg 2001; Valentino, Hutchings, and White 2002; Valentino, Traugott, and Hutchings 2002; Hurwitz and Peffley 2005; White 2007). Finally, a number of studies have found that messages from African American elites are more influential in shaping how Blacks interpret events than messages from elites who do not share this identity (Kuklinski and Hurley 1994; Kuklinski and Hurley 1996; Domke et al. 2000; Nelson et al. 2007).

Given the well-documented influence of elite actors in shaping public opinion the key question, of course, becomes who are these elites? To put it bluntly, elite approaches are likely to adopt a rather restrictive definition of elites that reserves influence only for those who engage primarily in political activity. Elite opinion theory's leading scholar, John Zaller, for example, defines elites as "persons who devote themselves full time to some aspect of politics or public affairs . . . these elites include politicians, higher level government officials, journalists, some activists and many kinds of experts and policy specialists" (Zaller 1992, 6). Similarly, Carmines and Kuklinski (1990) draw a distinction between elites, "those whose primary business is governing the nation" and non-elites, "those for whom politics is secondary" (9). Whatever the specific definition, the main point here is that the elite opinion theory restricts its focus to political elites and, as a result, rules out the influence of non-political elites through definitional fiat.

While narrow definitions of "elites" such as the ones provided above are relatively standard fare in studies of national public opinion, they are insufficiently inclusive to accurately assess the dynamics of attitude change in minority communities. The necessity of employing an even wider conception of "elites" stems in large measure from the fact that there are relatively few members of minority groups who occupy positions of power in formal political institutions. For instance, in the 111th Congress, there are forty-three African American members of the House of Representatives and one African American Senator who made up only 8 percent of the total congressional membership while there were roughly 455 non-Hispanic Whites who make up close to 86 percent of Congress.[5] If members of minority groups are likely to look to leaders who share their racial or ethnic background for guidance about political issues, therefore, they are probably looking beyond the halls of Congress. As a result, Lee (2002) and McClain et al. (2008) argue that studies of opinion dynamics within minority communities must define "elites" in a way that includes not only political actors who are part of the formal institutions of local, state, and national government, but also individuals, such as community organizers, church leaders, media personalities, and heads of interest groups, who have historically been influential by operating outside of these channels (Gaines 1997; Cohen 1999; Dawson 2001; Harris-Lacewell 2004).[6]

Unfortunately, there has been very little research assessing the impact that these less traditional elites have on public opinion within the Black community. In particular, empirical work has infrequently addressed the role that African American clergy play in guiding the political opinions of their congregations.[7] This is not to suggest, of course, that the influence of Black church leaders has been ignored in the literature on Black politics. Numerous scholarly assessments have shown that African American religious elites are important in mobilizing political action (McAdam 1982; Morris 1984; Lincoln and Mamiya 1990; Tate 1993; Brown and Wolford 1994; Calhoun-Brown 1996, 1999;

Harris 1999; Brown 2001; McKenzie 2004), increasing support for gender equality (Wilcox and Thomas 1992; Calhoun-Brown 1996) and fostering stronger perceptions of racial identity (Shingles 1981; McClerking 2001; Harris-Lacewell 2004) among Blacks. Studies seeking to examine the impact of church attendance and clergy messages on African American public opinion, however, have been few and far between.

Hypotheses

In this paper, we test two fairly straightforward hypotheses regarding African Americans' perceptions of commonality with Latinos culled from the predictions of elite opinion theory and the aforementioned statements of African American religious leaders on this issue.

> H1: African Americans who are exposed to messages in their places of worship regarding race relations will express more commonality with Latinos than African Americans who are not exposed to such messages.
> H2: The measure of exposure to messages regarding race relations will predict African American opinion toward commonality with Latinos even after controlling for all other potential influences on African American opinion.

Data and Measures

In order to test our hypotheses regarding the influence of elite messages on African American perceptions of commonality with Latinos we employ the 2004 National Politics Study (NPS) sponsored by the University of Michigan's Institute for Social Research. The NPS uses random digit dialed sample of residents of the United States aged eighteen years or older to gauge their opinions on a range of topics. Interviews were completed by telephone in both English and Spanish between September 2004 and February 2005 among a sample of 3,339.

Given the focus on social, economic, and political similarities between Latinos and African Americans in the messages articulated by members of the African American clergy, the dependent variables in our analysis are three measures of commonality between the two groups. The first item asks "how close do you feel to Hispanics in your ideas, interests, and feelings about things?" The second item asks respondents if "the problems of Blacks, Hispanics, and Asian Americans are too different for them to be political allies or partners." The final item asks respondents if Hispanics face "a lot of discrimination, some, a little, or no discrimination at all?" We include this final item because previous scholarship has found that both Latinos and African Americans believe they are victims of racial discrimination. In addition, much of the rhetoric of African American religious elites on relations between Latinos and African Americans stresses a common experience with racial discrimination. Each item was scaled from 0 to 1, with 1 representing strong support for perceptions of commonality (i.e., feel close, problems are similar, face a lot of discrimination), and 0 representing weak perceptions of commonality between the two groups.

We include in each of our models a set of theoretically important variables that have been shown to be important determinants of African American attitudes toward Latinos in previous research. Contact with Latinos is measured with items that ask respondents to describe the ethnic mix of their group of friends. Proximity to Latinos is measured with an item that asks respondents to describe the ethnic mix of their current neighborhoods.[8] Perceptions of competition with African Americans are measured with an index containing two items, the belief that better jobs or influence in politics for Latinos means fewer jobs or less influence in politics for African Americans.[9] Linked fate is measured with an item that asks respondents if they believe what happens "generally to African American people in this country will have something to do with what happens in your life." We also include a measure of group consciousness among African Americans with an item that asks respondents if they feel close in their ideas, interests, and feelings with other African Americans.[10] Support for Latino stereotypes is measured with an item that asks respondents if Latinos are hardworking or lazy.[11]

In order to control for the impact of religiosity on attitudes toward commonality we include an item that asks how often respondents attended religious services.[12] We also include items that measure a respondent's religious affiliation and, given that a plurality of African American respondents identify as Baptist (46 percent), we include a measure of Baptist religious identification. We also examine the impact of the religious demographics of a respondent's church with an item that taps whether or not a respondent attends a mostly African American church. Finally, in line with the literature on Latino commonality with African Americans, we include items that tap African Americans' perceptions of closeness with Whites, Asians, and Caribbeans in order to control for out-group receptivity on perceptions of commonality with African Americans (*see* Kaufmann 2003; Rodrigues and Segura 2003).[13]

Our primary explanatory variable of interest measures whether or not a respondent was exposed to a message from a religious leader on the issue of race relations. The item asks respondents: "During the past year have you heard a sermon, lecture, or discussion at your place of worship that dealt with improving relations between members of different racial or ethnic groups?" Unfortunately, this measure is an imperfect instrument for assessing the influence of clergy messages on the racial attitudes of parishioners. The measure has two limitations in particular. First, the question asked in the NPS does not reveal anything about whether the sermon, lecture, or discussion heard by a respondent emphasized a positive or negative view of the relations between African Americans and Latinos. Second, the question does not directly identify the source of the sermon, lecture, or discussion and, as a result, makes it impossible to determine whether the clergy, fellow parishioners, or some other actor was responsible for the message being communicated.

Despite these limitations, we believe the NPS question provides an acceptable measure of exposure to clergy messages in favor of positive assessments of the relations between African Americans and Latinos. As suggested above, a number of prominent African American clergy members have publicly stated their support for linkages between the African American and Latino communities. Of course, it is not necessarily the case that pronouncements made by prominent African American religious leaders are followed by clergy at the local level. We know, however, of no empirical studies that show a large disconnect between pronouncements made by nationally recognized religious leaders and their local counterparts. In short, although we have a well-grounded sense of what African American religious elites at the national level are saying regarding relations between African Americans and Latinos, our understanding of the specific nature of local clergy comments is somewhat obscured by an absence of systematic research.

We are not the first to encounter these problems in an attempt to parse out the influence of religious leaders. Previous research has addressed the absence of good data about the specific content of clergy speeches by simply assuming that religious leaders from a particular denomination are communicating a certain kind of political message on the issues being studied (Fetzer 2001; Bjarnason and Welch 2004; Djupe and Hunt 2009). In the absence of any specific evidence to suggest that local clergy are breaking with prominent clergy leaders on perceptions of race relations, we follow the lead of previous research and assume (1) that the messages are being communicated by local religious leaders (such as those seen in Table 1) and (2) that the messages are supportive of clear commonalities between the status of African Americans and Latinos. It is important to point out, however, that these assumptions may stack the deck against our hypothesis that exposure to messages on improving race relations matter for the racial attitudes of African American congregation members. Indeed, if clergy do exert an influence over parishioner attitudes and are frequently breaking ranks with the nationally prominent leaders on the question of commonality with Latinos, the lack of precision in the NPS measure will produce insignificant results in the statistical analyses we conduct. To the extent that we find evidence that this imperfect measure of exposure increases support for perceptions of commonality, our argument about the influence of religious elites will be bolstered.

Moreover, we believe that even with its imperfections, this NPS question is an obvious improvement over the variables that are typically used in public opinion research to assess the influence of exposure to elite messages. Indeed, cross-sectional studies of elite effects on public opinion have typically relied on proxy measures of exposure to elite communications such as a respondent's level of political knowledge (Zaller 1992; Price and Zaller 1993; Delli Carpini and Keeter 1996) or education (Popkin 1991; Sniderman, Brody, and Tetlock 1991). The measure of exposure found in the NPS, unlike the use of these proxy indicators, more directly assesses whether respondents were actually exposed to a message on race relations and more concretely pinpoints the location in which these messages were received.

Results

A number of studies have demonstrated that the African American clergy frequently speak to their congregations about interracial relations (Calhoun-Brown 1996; Harris 1999; McDaniel 2003). Consistent with the findings from these studies, a majority of African Americans in the 2004 National Politics Survey (60 percent) reported hearing a sermon, lecture, or discussion on improving relations between racial and ethnic groups at their places of worship. As Table 2 shows, exposure to messages about race relations in churches was more common than exposure to messages on a wide range of topics—including immigration, the situation in Iraq, terrorism, the legal system, and police. In fact, the only category of topics that are discussed more frequently in churches according to African American respondents was jobs, the economy, and poverty. As Table 2 also shows, African Americans are far more likely than Whites, Latinos, or Asians to hear some discussion on race relations in their places of worship. In other words, African American churches appear to be both strongly and uniquely focused on communicating to their members the importance of improving the African American community's relationship with other racial and ethnic groups.

Table 2.
Percent Exposed to Messages on Political Topics in Places of Worship by Race

	African American	White	Latino	Asian
Jobs, the economy or the poor	63%	49%	45%	45%
Improving relations between members of different racial or ethnic groups	60%	56%	50%	48%
Situation in Iraq or terrorism	57%	46%	51%	48%
Legal system or the police	36%	11%	18%	16%
Immigration or immigrants	15%	12%	34%	24%

Note: Entries are percentages of respondents by race who reported exposure to a message on the topic.
Source: National Politics Survey (2004).

We hypothesized that African Americans who were exposed to messages on race relations in their places of worship will express a stronger sense of commonality with Latinos than others who are not similarly exposed to these messages in their places of worship (H1). As Table 3 shows, African Americans who were exposed to a message on improving race relations were more likely to believe perceive commonality between African Americans and Latinos. More specifically, African Americans who were exposed to a message on race relations were more likely to believe that African Americans and Latinos are very close or fairly close in their ideas, interests, and feelings about things when compared to African Americans who were not exposed to such messages. Additionally, African Americans who were exposed to a positive message on race relations are also more likely to believe that Latinos are victims of racial discrimination and that African Americans, Latinos, and Asians share political interests that can be used as the basis for coalitions. Chi-square tests of independence reveal that the differences between African American parishioners who reported hearing a message on race relations and those who did not were statistically significant for each of the dependent variables under analysis.

Although the results of chi-square tests provide initial evidence that messages from religious elites influence the way African Americans think about their relationship with Latinos, a more sophisticated analysis is needed to control for the influence that other factors may have on perceptions of commonality. As a result, we use ordinary least squares (OLS) regression to predict responses to our measures of commonality with Latinos. As Model 1 in Table 4 shows, African American perceptions of closeness with Latinos grow from a relatively small number of sources that, overall, do a very good job at explaining the dependent variable (with an adjusted R^2 of .45). First, closeness to other minority groups is a major influence on African American feelings toward Latinos. More specifically, we find that African American perceptions of closeness with other racial minorities, notably Asians and Caribbeans, have a positive impact on African American perceptions of closeness to Latinos. Second, perceptions of closeness with African Americans and linked fate with Blacks both have a positive impact on perceptions of closeness with Latinos. We also uncover that economic considerations play an important role in accounting for African American perceptions of closeness with Latinos. African Americans who are unemployed

Table 3.
African American Opinion on Commonality with Latinos

How Close Do You Feel Toward Latinos (N=730)

	Very Close	Fairly Close	Not Too Close	Not Close At All
Exposed	18%	57%	17%	9%
Not Exposed	16%	47%	24%	14%
(N)	(122)	(380)	(146)	(82)
Chi-squared				12.17**

Discrimination Against Latinos (N=742)

	A Lot	Some	A Little	None
Exposed	36%	52%	11%	1%
Not Exposed	33%	50%	12%	5%
(N)	(256)	(378)	(84)	(24)
Chi-squared				10.62**

Political Commonality with Latinos and Asians (N=729)

	Strongly Agree	Somewhat Agree	Somewhat Disagree	Strongly Disagree
Exposed	54%	19%	17%	10%
Not Exposed	43%	26%	15%	15%
(N)	(356)	(164)	(117)	(92)
Chi-squared				12.73**

Note: Entries are percentages of respondents who expressed opinion on issue.
*** $p < .001$ ** $p < .01$ * $p < .05$
Source: National Politics Survey (2004).

and African Americans who see high levels of competition with Latinos perceive greater distance with the Latino community. Finally, we find that African Americans that hold negative stereotypes of Latinos, older African Americans, and African Americans who live in the South all express less positive views of closeness with Latinos.

What role, if any, does religion play in accounting for African American opinion toward perceptions of closeness with Latinos? Interestingly, we find that frequent religious attendance does not predict African American opinion on commonality with Latinos, but religious identification as a Baptist has a negative relationship with opinion on closeness with Latinos. On the other hand, we find modest support for our expectation that African American religious elites influence African American opinion on commonality. More precisely, we find that African American respondents who were exposed to religious messages on improving race relations are more likely to believe that African Americans hold a stronger association with Latinos.

In order to further illustrate the impact of religious elites on perceptions of commonality with Latinos, we use a unique feature of the 2004 National Politics Survey. As suggested above, the survey not only probes respondents about their feelings of closeness with Latinos but also asks respondents if they perceive Latinos to be victims of racial discrimination and if they perceive political commonalities with Latinos (and Asians). It seems reasonable to assume that if messages on race relations are likely to predict perceptions of closeness with Latinos, that these same messages would positively influence African American opinion on measures of political and social commonality. Table 4 also includes OLS models that predict African American opinion toward perceptions of discrimination faced by Latinos as well as perceptions toward political commonalities with Latinos. As seen in Table 4, exposure to messages on improving race relations have a modest, but significant, influence on African American opinion toward discrimination against Latinos as well as perceptions of political commonality with Latinos. When coupled with the results presented in Table 3, these findings indicate that exposure to elite communications matter for how African Americans view their relationships with Latinos.

Table 4.
OLS Regressions for African American Perceptions of Commonality

	Closeness to Latinos	High Level of Latino Discrimination	Political Commonality
Age	–.12**	–.04	–.08
	(.05)	(.05)	(.08)
Income	–.05	–.00	.00
	(.03)	(.04)	(.05)
Male	.00	.05*	–.03
	(.02)	(.02)	(.03)
Education	–.00	.13**	.09
	(.04)	(.04)	(.06)
South	–.10***	–.01	–.04
	(.02)	(.02)	(.03)
Unemployed	–.08*	–.08+	–.04
	(.04)	(.05)	(.07)
Latino Neighborhood	.03	.02	.00
	(.02)	(.03)	(.04)
Latino Friends	.04	–.00	.03
	(.03)	(.03)	(.04)
Competition with Latinos	–.06**	–.01	–.16***
	(.02)	(.02)	(.04)
Linked Fate	.02+	.07**	.01
	(.02)	(.03)	(.04)
Closeness with Blacks	.26***	.17***	.01
	(.04)	(.05)	(.07)
Closeness with Asians	.33***	.07	.13*
	(.04)	(.05)	(.07)

(continued on next page)

Table 4. (*continued*)

	Closeness to Latinos	High Level of Latino Discrimination	Political Commonality
Closeness with Whites	−.01	−.08*	−.09
	(.04)	**(.04)**	(.06)
Closeness with Caribbeans	.19***	−.05	.05
	(.04)	(.04)	(.06)
Latinos are Lazy	−.11**	−.01	−.09
	(.04)	(.05)	(.07)
Religiosity	.00	.00	.08
	(.04)	(.05)	(.07)
Exposure to Message on Race Relations	.04*	.06**	.05+
	(.02)	**(.02)**	**(.03)**
Black Church	−.05	−.01	−.06
	(.03)	(.04)	(.05)
Baptist	−.06**	.00	.01
	(.02)	(.02)	(.03)
Constant	.33***	.50***	.71***
	(.06)	**(.07)**	**(.10)**
Standard Error	.20	.24	.35
Adjusted R-Square	.45	.09	.07
N	501	498	499

Notes: Figures listed are unstandardized regression coefficients.

Standard errors are in parenthesis.+ p<.10, *p<.05, **p<.01, ***p<.001

Source: National Politics Survey (2004).

Conclusion

What impact do messages from African American religious leaders regarding commonality with Latinos have on the African American community? This article finds support for our hypotheses regarding the role that religious elite messages play in the formulation of African American perceptions of commonality with Latinos. We interpret these descriptive and explanatory findings to indicate that elite discourse, particularly from members of the African American clergy, is an important component in the process by which African Americans form their opinions on commonality with Latinos.

The findings presented here make a number of key contributions to the literature on the African American church, public opinion, multiracial coalitions, and interracial conflict. First, unlike studies of African American racial views of Latinos that focus exclusively on individual level determinants of these attitudes, our study finds preliminary evidence that members of the African American clergy are sending positive messages regarding commonality with Latinos to their African American parishioners and that these signals subsequently influence the perceptions of commonality of African Americans exposed to these messages. Much of the current work on the relationship between the African American church and its parishioners focuses attention on the role of the church in facilitating political participation (Lincoln and Mamiya 1990; Tate 1993; Brown and Wolford 1994; Calhoun-Brown 1996, 1999; Harris 1999; McKenzie 2004). We hope the conclusions presented here help to expand the boundaries of the literature on the role of the African American church, and in particular the African American clergy, in shaping the contours of African American public opinion.

The second contribution that this study makes is to studies of public opinion more generally by testing the application of Zaller's model for a new population—African Americans—and for a new issue—commonality. There is an open question in the literature about how far elite influence will extend (Paul and Brown 2001). Most studies of elite influence have focused attention on issues that are abstract and complex based on the assumption that elite influence is greater on these issues given the public's proclivity for "rational ignorance" in the realm of politics. We find, however, that elite influence extends to perceptions of commonality with Latinos, an issue that African Americans can become easily informed about on their own and an issue that many African Americans have direct experiences with in their daily lives (Mindiola et al. 2002; Meier et al. 2004; Vaca 2004). It appears, therefore, that religious elites may have the ability to shape perceptions of everyday life by framing group dynamics in a particular fashion.

Third, these findings further expand our understanding of the role that elites may play in the formation of multiracial coalitions between America's two largest minority groups and the mitigation of conflict between these two communities over scarce resources (Johnson and Oliver 1989; McClain and Karnig 1990; Meier and Stewart 1991; Bobo and Hutchings 1996; Kaufman 2003; Meier et al. 2004; Vaca 2004; Rocha 2007). Studies of multiracial coalition formation have pointed to a number of conditions that are necessary to create successful multiracial coalitions—including shared interests, ideology, and circumstances (Browning, Marshall, and Tabb 1984; Sonenshein 1990, 2003). Although this literature has significantly expanded our knowledge about cooperation between African Americans and Latinos, much of the existing research tells us painfully little about the underlying attitudinal foundations upon which multiracial coalitions might be built. To be more precise, existing studies of multiracial coalitions between African Americans and Latinos focus too heavily on objective measures of socioeconomic, experiential, and partisan similarities and largely ignore the significant role that perceptions of commonality are likely to play in any effort to construct sustainable coalitions. We hope that the results of the analysis presented here will refocus attention on the importance of feelings of economic and political commonality in coalition formation and, more importantly, remind scholars of the importance of religious leadership in forging bonds of cooperation across racial and ethnic lines.

While we believe our findings make an initial and exploratory case for the importance of religious elite discourse in understanding the mass public's perception of race relations, we also believe that there is much more to be done. Future research should more systematically examine the content of elite messages (from both religious and political elites) regarding economic and political commonality with Latinos to get a more complete picture of the nature of elite rhetoric on this issue (e.g., whether there is a polarized or unified elite communication environment, whether the nature of elite discourse differs by region,

over time, or by religious denomination). Additionally, future work may seek to explain why influential members of the African American clergy seek to strengthen perceptions of commonality with Latinos among their parishioners. Given our reading of statements from Black clergy on this topic, we suspect that this rhetorical move reflects an attempt to alleviate increasing tensions between African American and Latino communities as well as the recognition that strengthening perceptions of commonality between the two communities increases the probability that the two groups may come together to help achieve their shared political and socioeconomic goals. However, definitive answers to this question are beyond the relatively narrow scope of this paper. We do hope that the findings presented here encourage future researchers to pursue in-depth interviews of the Black clergy and more rigorous content analysis of clergy messages on commonality.

In order to provide an encompassing portrait of the role of elites, future studies may also contribute to the work we have done here by examining the impact of elite messages on Latinos' perceptions of economic and political commonality with African Americans. In addition, future work in this literature should seek to develop more nuanced measures of commonality that reflect not only the social, political, and economic similarities between groups, but the philosophical aspects of commonality that speak to: a sense of belonging and identification with a collectivity that is important to members (i.e., minorities or people of color), a degree of mutual concern among members which is greater than that for human beings generally, a sense of linked fate, mutual trust, and loyalty (*see* Shelby 2005; Blum 2007). In order to better specify the causal relationship between elite messages and public opinion, future studies should employ experimental methods that better address issues of causality that arise in the use of cross sectional data.

At a minimum, we hope that scholars will replicate the kind of analysis we have done here with more recent data. The findings we have spelled out above suggest that church-based messages were essential for understanding the ways that the African American community evaluated their relationship with Latinos in 2004. In the seven years since these data were collected, however, the political environment has evolved in ways that are likely to have far reaching, yet unpredictable, consequences for the power of elite rhetoric on intergroup relations. It is probable, for example, that the growing number of Latinos in southern states, the Congressional Black Caucus's support for comprehensive immigration reform, Barack Obama's election in 2008, and the enactment of strict anti-immigration laws in places like Arizona and Alabama altered the national political landscape in ways that have transformed the importance of political leadership on race relations. Until work on developments such as these is done, a definitive understanding of whether the separate struggles of African Americans and Latinos are indeed one will remain elusive.

Notes

*   In this paper we use the terms African American and Black interchangeably. The term represents native born citizens of the United States who self-identify as African American in the 2004 National Politics Study.

1.   In 2003, the Latino population made up more than 16 percent of the total U.S. population (fifty million) while African Americans accounted for 12 percent of the total population (thirty-nine million).

2.   The quotes from members of the African American clergy were taken from a search of LexisNexis newspaper articles on relations between African Americans and Latinos.

3. In the 2004 National Politics Study, Blacks were more likely than non-Blacks to claim they were "very religious" or "fairly religious" (90 percent to 81 percent) and equally likely as non-Blacks to attend church at least once a week (66 percent). According to a more recent study by the Pew Center (Sahgal and Smith 2009), African Americans were more likely than the US public: to believe religion was important in their lives (79 percent to 56 percent), to attend religious services frequently (53 percent to 36 percent), and to interpret Scripture as the literal word of God (55 percent to 33 percent).

4. A representative sample works that adopt an elite perspective on mass opinion can be found in Carmines and Stimson (1989); Brody (1991); Popkin (1991); Page and Shapiro (1992); Zaller (1992); Gerber and Jackson (1993); Karp (1998); Lupia and McCubbins (1998); and Erikson, MacKuen, and Stimson (2003). For a critique of elite opinion theories, see Lee (2002).

5. In comparison, Latinos hold 5 percent, Asian Americans 1.25 percent, and Native Americans less than 1 percent of the total congressional makeup.

6. All of the individuals quoted in Table 1 fit the requirements spelled out by Lee (2002) and McClain et al. (2008) quite well, and as a result we are confident that the proclamations of the above religious elites accurately represent African American elite viewpoints on commonality.

7. Studies that focus on the effects of the clergy on the opinion of White churchgoers have found mixed results, with some uncovering significant effects (Fetzer 2001; Bjarnasson and Welch 2004) and others discovering that religious leaders have very little impact on the opinion of their parishioners (Campbell and Monson 2003; Djupe and Gwiasda 2010). Unfortunately, the bulk of this literature focuses attention on the impact of political messages from the White clergy on their White congregations leaving the impact of African American clergy on opinions of their largely African American congregations unclear.

8. Each item is scaled from 0 to 1, with 1 indicating that a respondent has mostly Latino friends and lives in a mostly Latino neighborhood.

9. The Cronbach's Alpha for this index is 0.60.

10. Both items were measured from 0 to 1, with 1 indicating strong support for a linked fate or group consciousness viewpoint.

11. This is also measured from 0 to 1, with 1 indicating that a respondent views Latinos as lazy and 0 represents a respondent's viewing of Latinos as hardworking.

12. This variable is measured from 0 to 1, with 1 representing daily attendance and 0 representing attendance a few times a year.

13. The model also controls for age, family income, sex, education, and region of residence.

References

Berelson, Bernard, Paul Lazarsfeld, and William McPhee. 1954. *Voting: A Study of Opinion Formation in a Presidential Campaign.* Chicago, IL: University of Chicago Press.

Bjarnason, Thoroddur, and Michael Welch. 2004. "Father Knows Best: Parishes, Priests, and American Catholic Parishioners' Attitudes toward Capital Punishment." *Journal for the Scientific Study of Religion* 43, no. 1: 103–18.

Blum, Lawrence. 2007. "Three Kinds of Race-Related Solidarity." *Journal of Social Philosophy* 38, no. 1: 53–72.

Bobo, Lawrence, and Vincent L. Hutchings. 1996. "Perceptions of Racial Group Competition: Extending Blumer's Theory of Group Position to a Multiracial Social Context." *American Sociological Review* 61, no. 6: 951–72.

Brody, Richard A. 1991. *Assessing the President: The Media, Elite Opinion, and Public Support.* Stanford, CA: Stanford University Press.

Brown, Ronald, and Monica L. Wolford. 1994. "Religious Resources and African-American Political Action." *The National Political Science Review* 4: 30–48.

Browning, Rufus, Dale Rogers Marshall, and David Tabb. 1984. *Protest Is Not Enough: The Struggle of African Americans and Hispanics for Equality in Urban Politics.* Berkeley: University of California Press.

Calhoun-Brown, Allison. 1996. "African-American Churches and Political Mobilization: The Psychological Impact of Organizational Resources." *Journal of Politics* 58, no. 4: 935–53.

———. 1997. "Still Seeing in Black and White: Racial Challenges for the Christian Right." In *Sojourners in the Wilderness: The Christian Right in Comparative Perspective*, ed. Corwin E. Smidt and James M. Penning, 115–38. Lanham, MD: Rowman & Littlefield.

———. 1999. "The Image of God: Black Theology and Racial Empowerment in the African American Community." *Review of Religious Research* 40, no. 3: 197–212.

Carmines, Edward G., and James H. Kuklinski. 1990. "Incentives, Opportunities, and the Logic of Public Opinion in American Political Representation." In *Information and Democratic Processes*, ed. John A. Ferejohn and James H. Kuklinski. Urbana, IL: University of Illinois Press.

Carmines, Edward G., and James A. Stimson. 1980. "The Two Faces of Issue Voting." *The American Political Science Review* 74, no. 1: 78–97.

———. 1991. *Issue Evolution: Race and the Transformation of American Politics*. Princeton, NJ: Princeton University Press.

Cohen, Cathy. 1999. *Boundaries of Blackness: AIDS and the Breakdown of Black Politics*. Chicago: University of Chicago Press.

Cummings, Scott, and Thomas Lambert. 1997. "Anti-Hispanic and Anti-Asian Sentiments among African Americans." *Social Science Quarterly* 78, no. 2: 338–53.

Dawson, Michael C., Ronald E. Brown, and Richard L. Allen. 1990. "Racial Belief Systems, Religious Guidance, and African American Political Participation." *National Review of Political Science* 2: 22–44.

Dawson, Michael. 2001. *Black Visions: The Roots of Contemporary African-American Political Ideologies*. Chicago, IL: University of Chicago Press.

Delli Carpini, Michael X., and Scott Keeter. 1996. *What Americans Know about Politics and Why It Matters*. New Haven, CT: Yale University Press.

Djupe, Paul A., and Christopher P. Gilbert. 2008. "Politics and Church: Byproduct or Central Mission?" *Journal for the Scientific Study of Religion* 47, no. 1: 45–62.

Djupe, Paul A., and G.W. Gwiasda. 2010. "Evangelizing the Environment: Decision Process Effects in Political Persuasion." *Journal for the Scientific Study of Religion* 49, no. 1: 73–86.

Djupe, Paul A., and Patrick K. Hunt. 2009. "Beyond the Lynn White Thesis: Congregational Effects on Environmental Concern." *Journal of the Scientific Study of Religion* 48, no. 4: 670–86.

Domke, D., T. Lagos, M. LaPointe, M. Meade, and M. A. Xenos. 2000. Elite Messages and Source Cues: Moving Beyond Partisanship. *Political Communication* 17, no. 4: 395–402.

Downs, Anthony. 1957. *An Economic Theory of Democracy*. New York: Harper & Bros.

Erikson, Robert, Michael B. MacKuen, and James Stimson. 2002. *The Macro Polity*. New York: Cambridge University Press.

Fetzer, J. S. 2001. "Shaping Pacifism: The Role of the Local Anabaptist Pastor." In *Christian Clergy in American Politics*, ed. S.E.S. Crawford and L.R. Olson. Baltimore, MD: Johns Hopkins University Press.

Gaines, Kevin. 1997. *Uplifting the Race: Black Leadership, Politics, and Culture in the Twentieth Century*. Chapel Hill, NC: University of North Carolina Press.

Gay, Claudine. 2006. "Seeing Difference: The Effect of Economic Disparity on Black Attitudes toward Latinos." *American Journal of Political Science* 50, no. 4: 982–97.

Gerber, Elisabeth R., and John E. Jackson. 1993. "Endogenous Preferences and the Study of Institutions." *American Political Science Review* 87, no. 3: 639–56.

Giles, Michael W., and Arthur S. Evans. 1985. "External Threat, Perceived Threat, and Group Identity." *Social Science Quarterly* 66, no. 1: 50–66.

Harris, Fredrick. 1999. *Something Within: Religion in African American Political Activism*. New York: Oxford University Press.

Harris-Lacewell, Melissa. 2004. *Barbershops, Bibles, and B.E.T. Everyday Talk and Black Political Thought*. Princeton, NJ: Princeton University Press.

Herrera, Kevin. 2005. "Is Illegal Immigration the Sticking Point?" *Wave West* 88, no. 31: 1, 12.

Hurwitz, Jon, and Mark Peffley. 2005. "Playing the Race Card in the Post-Willie Horton Era: The Impact of Racialized Code Words on Support for Punitive Crime Policy." *Public Opinion Quarterly* 69, no. 1: 99–112.

Jackson, Bryan, Elizabeth Gerber, and Bruce Cain. 1994. "Coalitional Prospects in a Multiracial Society: African American Attitudes toward Other Minority Groups." *Political Research Quarterly* 47: 277–94.

Jones, Clarence, and Joel Engel. 2008. *What Would Martin Say?* Mount Vernon, VA: HarperCollins.

Johnson, James H., and Melvin Oliver. 1989. "Interethnic Minority Conflict in Urban America: The Effects of Economic and Social Dislocations." *Urban Geography* 10, no. 5: 449–63.

Karp, Jeffrey A. 1998. "The Influence of Elite Endorsements in Initiative Campaigns." In *Citizens as Legislators*, ed. Shaun Bowler, Todd Donovan, and Caroline Tolbert, 149–65. Ohio University Press.

Kaufmann, Karen M. 2003. "Cracks in the Rainbow: Group Commonality as a Basis for Latino and African-American Political Coalitions." *Political Research Quarterly* 56, no. 2: 199–210.

Kuklinski, James H., and Norman L. Hurley. 1994. "On Hearing and Interpreting Political Messages: A Cautionary Tale of Citizen Cue-Taking." *Journal of Politics* 56, no. 3: 729–51.

———. 1996. "It's a Matter of Interpretation." In *Political Persuasion and Attitude Change*, ed. D.M. Muntz, P.M. Sniderman, and R. Brody. Ann Arbor: University of Michigan Press.

Lee, Taeku. 2002. *Mobilizing Public Opinion: Black Insurgency and Racial Attitudes in the Civil Rights Movement.* Chicago, IL: University of Chicago Press.

Lincoln, C. Eric, and Lawrence H. Mamiya, eds. 1999. *The Black Church in the African American Experience.* Durham, NC: Duke University Press.

Lovato, Robert. "Undocumented Immigrants Face Juan Crow." *The Progressive.* May 14, 2008. 1.

Lupia, Arthur, and Mathew D. McCubbins. 1998. *The Democratic Dilemma: Can Citizens Learn What They Need to Know?* Cambridge, UK: Cambridge University Press.

McAdam, Doug. 1982. *Political Process and the Development of African American Insurgency, 1930–1970.* Chicago, IL: University of Chicago Press.

McClain, Paula, and Albert Karnig. 1990. "Black and Hispanic Socioeconomic and Political Competition." *American Political Science Review* 84, no. 2: 535–45.

McClain, Paula, Monique Lyle, Niambi Carter, Victoria DeFrancesco Soto, Gerald Lackey, Kendra Cotton, Shayla Nunnally, Thomas Scotto, Jeffrey Grynaviski, J. Alan Kendrick. 2007. "Black Americans and Latino Immigrants in a Southern City: Friendly Neighbors or Economic Competitors?" *Du Bois Review* 4, no. 1: 97–117.

———. 2008. "Black Elites and Latino Immigrant Relations in a Southern City: Do Black Elites and the Black Masses Agree?" In *New Race Politics in America: Understanding Minority and Immigrant Populations*, ed. Jane Junn and Kerry Haynie. Cambridge, MA: Cambridge University Press.

McClerking, Howard K. 2001. *We Are in This Together.* Ph.D. diss., University of Michigan.

McDaniel, Eric. 2003. "Black Clergy in the 2000 Election." *Journal for the Scientific Study of Religion* 42, no. 4: 533–46.

McDaniel, Eric, and Christopher G. Ellison. 2008. "God's Party? Race, Religion, and Partisanship over Time." *Political Research Quarterly* 61, no. 2: 180–91.

McKenzie, Brian D. 2004. "Religious Social Networks, Indirect Mobilization, and African-American Political Participation." *Political Research Quarterly* 57, no. 4: 621–32.

Meier, Kenneth, and Stewart, Joseph. 1991. "Cooperation and Conflict in Multiracial School Districts." *Journal of Politics* 53, no. 4: 1123–33.

Meier, Kenneth J., Paula D. McClain, J. L. Polinard, and Robert D. Wrinkle. 2004. "Divided or Together? Conflict and Cooperation between African Americans and Latinos." *Political Research Quarterly* 57, no. 3: 399–409.

Melvin, Lindsay. "Churches Seek Unity of Black and Hispanic Communities." *The Commercial Appeal.* April 21, 2008. 1.

Mendelberg, Tali. 2001. *The Race Card: Campaign Strategy, Implicit Messages, and the Norm of Equality.* Princeton, NJ: Princeton University Press.

Mindiola, Tatch, Yolanda Flores Niemann, and Nestor Rodriguez. 2002. *African American-Brown Relations and Stereotypes.* Austin, TX: University of Texas Press.

Morris, Aldon. 1984. *The Origins of the Civil Rights Movement: African American Communities Organizing for Change.* New York: Free Press.

National Hispanic Christian Leadership Conference (NHCLC). "Christian Leaders Call on President Obama to Lead the Immigration Reform Debate." June 10, 2009.

Nelson, Thomas, Kira Sanbonmatsu, and Harwood K. McClerking. 2007. "Playing a Different Race Card: Examining the Limits of Elite Influence on Perceptions of Racism. *The Journal of Politics* 69: 416–29.

Niemann, Y. F. 1999. "Social Ecological Contexts and Prejudice between Hispanics and African Americans." In *Race, Ethnicity, and Nationality in the United States: Toward the Twenty-First Century*, ed. P. Wong. Boulder, CO: Westview Press.

Niemann, Y. F., L. Jennings, R. M. Rozelle, J. C. Baxter, and E. Sullivan. 1994. "Use of Free Response and Cluster Analysis to Determine Stereotypes of Eight Groups." *Personality and Social Psychology Bulletin* 20, no. 4: 379–90.

O'Brien, Matt. "African American Churches in the East Bay Give Immigrants Voice." *Contra Costa Times.* September 7, 2009. 1.

Oliver, J. Eric, and Janelle Wong. 2003. "Intergroup Prejudice in Multiethnic Settings." *American Journal of Political Science* 47, no. 4: 567–82.

Page, Benjamin, and Robert Shapiro. 1992. *The Rational Public: Fifty Years of Trends in Americans' Policy Preferences.* Chicago, IL: University of Chicago Press.

Paul, David, and Clyde Brown. 2001. "Testing the Limits of Elite Influence on Public Opinion: An Examination of Sports Facility Referendums." *Political Research Quarterly*, 54, no. 4: 871–88.

Poole, Shelia. "Shades of the Immigration Debate." *The Atlanta Journal Constitution*. May 10, 2006. 1F

Popkin, Samuel L. 1991. *The Reasoning Voter: Communication and Persuasion in Presidential Campaigns*. Chicago, IL: University of Chicago Press.

Price, Vincent, and John Zaller. 1993. "Who Gets the News? Alternative Measures of News Reception and Their Implications for Research." *Public Opinion Quarterly* 57, no. 2 (Summer): 133–64.

Reese, Laura, and Ronald E. Brown. 1995. The Effects, of Religious Messages on Racial Identity and System Blame among African Americans. *The Journal of Politics* 57: 24–43.

Regester, Yasmine. "Bringing Blacks & Hispanics Together." *Carolina Peacemaker*. September 18, 2008. 1A.

Riley, Jennifer. "Faith Leaders Back Obama on Immigration Reform." *The Christian Post*. July 1, 2010. 1.

Rocha, Rene R. 2007. "Black-Brown Coalitions in Local School Board Elections." Political Research Quarterly, 60, no.2: 315–27

Rodrigues, Helena, and Gary Segura. 2003. "Attitudinal Underpinnings of African American-Brown Coalitions: Latino Perceptions of Commonality with African Americans and Anglos." Unpublished paper.

Sahgal, Neha, and Greg Smith. 2009. "A Religious Portrait of African Americans." *The Pew Forum on Religion & Public Life*. Washington, D.C.

Sanchez, Gabriel. 2008. "Latino Group Consciousness and Perceptions of Commonality with African Americans." *Social Science Quarterly* 89, no. 2: 428–44.

Shelby, Tommie. 2005. *We Who Are Dark*. Cambridge, MA: Harvard University Press.

Shingles, Richard D. 1981. "Black Consciousness and Political Participation: The Missing Link." *American Political Science Review* 75: 76–91.

Sniderman, Paul M., Richard A. Brody, and Philip E. Tetlock. 1991. *Reasoning and Choice: Explorations in Political Psychology*. Cambridge, MA: Cambridge University Press.

Sonenshein, Raphael J. 1990. "Biracial Coalition Politics in Los Angeles." In *Racial Politics in American Cities*, ed. Rufus P. Browning, Dale Rogers Marshall, and David H. Tabb. New York: Longman.

———. 1993. *Politics in Black and White: Race and Power in Los Angeles*. Princeton, NJ: Princeton University Press.

———. 2003. "The Prospects for Multiracial Coalitions: Lessons from America's Three Largest Cities." In *Racial Politics in American Cities*, ed. Rufus P. Browning, Dale Rogers Marshall, and David H. Tabb. New York: Longman.

Tate, Katherine. 1993. *From Protest to Politics: The New African American Voters in American Elections*. Cambridge, MA: Harvard University Press.

Thornton, Michael, and Yuko Mizuno. 1999. "Economic Well-Being and Black Adult Feelings toward Immigrants and Whites, 1984." *Journal of African American Studies* 30: 15–44.

Vaca, Nicolas. 2004. *The Presumed Alliance: The Unspoken Conflict between Latinos and African Americans and What It Means for America*. New York: Harper Collins.

Valentino, Nicholas, Vincent Hutchings, and Ismail White. 2002. "Cues that Matter: How Political Ads Prime Racial Attitudes During Campaigns." *American Political Science Review* 96, no. 1: 75–90.

Valentino, Nicholas A., Michael Traugott, and Vincent L. Hutchings. 2002. "Group Cues and Ideological Constraint: A Replication of Political Advertising Effects Studies in the Lab and in the Field." *Political Communication* 19, no. 1: 29–48.

Verba, Sidney, Kay Schlozman, and Henry Brady. 1995. *Voice and Equality: Civic Voluntarism in American Politics*. Cambridge, MA: Harvard University Press.

Walton, Hanes, Jr. 1985. *Invisible Politics: African American Political Behavior*. Albany, NY: State University of New York Press.

Welch, Michael R., David C. Leege, Kenneth D. Wald, and Lyman A. Kellstedt. 1993. "Are the Sheep Hearing the Shepards? Cue Perceptions, Congregational Responses, and Political Communication Processes." In *Rediscovering the Religious Factor in American Politics*, ed. Leege, David C. and Kellstedt, Lyman A. Armonk, NY: M.E. Sharpe.

Wilcox, Clyde, and Sue Thomas. 1992. "Religion and Feminist Attitudes among African- American Women: A View from the Nation's Capitol." *Women and Politics* 12, no. 2: 19–40.

White, Ismail. 2007. "When Race Matters and When It Doesn't: Racial Group Differences in Response to Racial Cues." *American Political Science Review* 101: 339–54.

Zaller, John. 1992. *The Nature and Origins of Mass Opinion*. Cambridge, UK: Cambridge University Press.

Appendix A

Age

What is the month, day, and year of your birth?

Family Income

Thinking about you and your family's total income for all sources, how much did you and all the members of your family living with you receive in the year 2003 before taxes?

Education

What is the highest grade or level of school that you have completed?

Unemployed

Are you working now full- or part-time, temporarily laid off, unemployed, on maternity or sick leave, retired, a homemaker, a student, permanently disabled, or something else?

Ideology

If you had to choose, would you consider yourself a liberal or a conservative?

Partisan Identification

Generally speaking, do you usually think of yourself as a republican, a democrat, an independent, or what?

Latino Neighborhood

How would you describe the ethnic mix of your current neighborhood where you live?

Latino Friends

How would you describe the ethnic mix of your group of friends?

Latino Competition

How much do you agree that more good jobs for Hispanics means fewer good jobs for people like you?

How much do you agree that the more influence Hispanics have in politics, the less influence people like you will have in politics?

Linked Fate

Do you think what happens generally to [R RACE] people in this country will have something to do with what happens in your life?

Closeness

Now I have some more questions about different groups in our society. How close do you feel to each of the following groups of people in your ideas, interests, and feelings about things? Very close, fairly close, not too close, or not close at all? (White people, African Americans, Asian Americans, Caribbeans)

Latinos Lazy

Where would you rate Hispanics in general on a scale of 1 to 7, where 1 indicates lazy, 7 means hardworking, and 4 indicates most Hispanics are not closer to one end or the other?

Dependent Variables

How close do you feel in your ideas, interests, and feelings to Hispanics?

Please indicate whether you strongly agree, somewhat agree, somewhat disagree, or strongly disagree with the following statements. The problems of Blacks, Hispanics, and Asian Americans are too different for them to be political allies or partners.

Do you think Hispanics face a lot of discrimination, some, a little, or no discrimination at all?

Religiosity

How often do you usually attend religious services?

Religious Preferences

What is your current religion or religious preference?

Exposure to Religious Elite Messages

During the past year, have you heard a sermon, lecture, or discussion at your place of worship that dealt with improving relations between members of different racial or ethnic groups?

Fighting for African American Interests in City Politics: Local Political Organizations and Black Political Efficacy

Micah W. Kubic
Howard University

Introduction

Since 1967, when Carl Stokes and Richard Hatcher became the first African American mayors of large American cities, increasing scholarly attention has been paid to the interplay between African Americans and local politics. Considerable effort has been exerted to determine whether the advent of African American mayoralties results in tangible benefits for the Black community and to identify the demographic conditions, alliances, and thematic emphases required for Black candidates to succeed. Existing scholarship tends to explain Black success in local electoral politics and at winning satisfaction of local systemic demands as the result of interracial coalitions, the charisma and political skills of individual leaders, or both. Failure in these same arenas is argued to be due to an inability to form or sustain interracial coalitions (usually blamed on "nationalist" or overly race-conscious elements within the Black community), factionalism and disunity among African Americans, the presence of an "urban regime" that views Black demands as a threat to its economic interests and so alternately squashes and co-opts Black community demands, or by the absence of political entrepreneurs who achieve success through wile and force of personality.

What goes largely unaddressed in the literature—regardless of the theoretical approach adopted—is the role that purely local political organizations and interest groups play in mediating these other tendencies, enabling or precluding Black electoral victory or policy success. Among the groups most neglected by this prevailing mode of analysis are local independent political clubs with targeted constituencies, which are referred to here as local political organizations (LPOs).[1] In non-partisan races, which include the majority of American big-city municipal elections, LPOs spring up to endorse candidates, mobilize voters, sponsor extensive advertising campaigns, and otherwise do the work that party committees perform in partisan races. In partisan ones, they represent the interests of a specific constituency within the party for the primary, serve as the liaison for the constituency to the party, and influence the turnout of the constituency in the general election.

Some lobby elected officials on issues of concern. Unlike political action committees (PACs), LPOs do more than endorse a candidate or make campaign donations; they do the real work of electioneering, including grassroots organizing and personal contact with voters. African American LPOs unify Black voters into a potent bloc capable of influencing elections and policy, especially in cities where African Americans are a minority confronted by a hostile or neglectful White majority.

The relative unimportance accorded to LPOs—especially African American LPOs—by the existing scholarly literature distorts our understanding of urban politics. This project presents a different view, by arguing that African American LPOs are vibrant, important political actors in their own right. The basic argument made here is that, in achieving political efficacy for African Americans in the urban context, institutions matter. Local-level Black political empowerment, collective agency, and political efficacy are not achieved primarily through individual campaigns for elective office, the charisma of individual candidates, or even the forging of alliances. At the local level, Black political empowerment, collective agency, and political efficacy are instead *best* achieved by the building of strong Black LPOs, ones that are independent of any individual candidate and which can credibly claim to "speak for" African Americans. This argument should *not* be misunderstood to mean that *all* Black political activity should take place within the confines of Black LPOs, or that interracial alliances are undesirable; it means instead that these modes of political activity are likely to be less efficacious unless they are accompanied by a strong Black LPO.

This article proceeds as follows. First, a short literature review is provided to demonstrate the relative lack of scholarly attention that has been paid to LPOs. Second, the theoretical argument made about the relationship between LPOs and Black political efficacy is more clearly defined and a method for evaluating the theory is developed. Finally, evidence for this argument is presented in the form of the results of a case study of Kansas City, Missouri, and its dominant Black LPO, Freedom, Inc.

Acknowledged but Ignored: A Review of Literature on LPOs

In studies of national politics, a thriving literature exists that treats organizations as actors in their own right rather than as mere instruments of the powerful. Literature on local politics, however, does not follow the same pattern, giving short shrift to formal organizations even as the field dwells at length on the contest for power between groups. "Machines" and the local incarnations of political parties have garnered some attention, but all manner of other local political organizations—including interest groups, slating organizations, voters' leagues, and even neighborhood associations—have not. When treated at all, formal groups are often portrayed as being reducible to labels such as "business interests" or "good government reformers" that are supposedly self-explanatory in behavior, motive, and constituency. These groups are regarded as being so generic as to demonstrate almost uniform behavior and motives across time and place. Little effort is made at examining how the internal politics of, activities of, or relationships between formal local organizations influence outcomes.

This omission is endemic to the four basic theoretical approaches to the study of urban politics. The institutional approach, associated primarily with the work of Edward Banfield and James Q. Wilson (Banfield 1965; Banfield and Wilson 1967), explains local political outcomes primarily through the governmental and electoral structures in place. Led by Banfield and Wilson, scholars working in this tradition acknowledge the interest groups that they argue recur in every city (including business interests, the local newspaper, "good government" types, and African Americans), but treat these organizations as largely interchangeable from one city to the next; only the names of the leaders and the organizations differ. The institutional approach values LPOs as political actors, but oversimplifies them as fixed, uniform, and predictable across time and space, not as living organisms that change in reaction to internal and external factors. This approach pre-dates the ascendance of Black political power in the cities, but treats the failure to win Black demands on the system as a product of either unreasonable demands or to broader structures, especially machine politics.

The political economy approach associated with Molotch's "growth machine" (1976) or Stone's "urban regime" (1989) is prescient in predicting a number of policy outcomes, tying those outcomes to the quest for economic growth by local policy-makers. These theories, too, give short shrift to individual organizations and enterprises which constitute the "regime" and are silent on what is to be expected when organized elements within the regime come into conflict with one another.

The highly popular electoral politics approach presumes that election results do reflect a community's coalitions, divisions, and power blocs. Within this approach, the hugely influential work of Browning, Marshall, and Tabb (1984, 1990, 2003) forcefully argues that Black interests can be served through participation in electoral politics and by crafting multiracial alliances. Their findings have inspired a cavalcade of similar research on the importance of interracial electoral alliances and "rainbow coalitions" in achieving Black progress in the urban context (Bent 1982; Mladenka 1989; Sonenshein 1989; Bobo and Gilliam 1990; Keiser and Underwood 2000; Hajnal 2001; Kaufmann 2003, 2004). Browning, Marshall, and Tabb acknowledge that interracial alliances are usually only possible after the Black community has achieved high degrees of internal unity, organization, and mobilization. This focus on Black unity and bloc voting as an essential component to Black electoral victories, given the context in which White racism continues to thrive and creates cities that are racially hyper-polarized, has been taken up by a number of other authors (Poinsett 1970; Alkalimat and Gills 1989; Pohlmann and Kirby 1996). Research in the electoral politics vein can be illuminating, because election results are usually the best available measure of genuine public opinion, but they occasionally veer into flattening political maneuvers into a single dimension that does not change until the next election. Lobbying, protest, shifting alliances, and changing public opinion are not reflected in the analysis until the next election comes along and the proverbial deck is reshuffled. This research approach fails to explain how elected officials evaluate the multitude of signals they receive about their re-election chances, or how they mediate conflicting claims about behavior that will influence those chances. Most problematically, the electoral approach views the inherently short-lived campaigns of would-be political officials as the most important unit of analysis. But campaigns do not exist in a vacuum and do not spring fully formed from the ether; instead, they tap into existing formal and informal infrastructures—in the form of LPOs, churches, and even casual networks of friends and acquaintances—and sometimes give birth to new ones on the road to success. These structures not only out-last the campaign, but influence the direction of multiple campaigns and policy contests simultaneously.

Surprisingly, the pressure groups approach follows this same general pattern. Neither the "community power structures" school associated with Hunter (Hunter 1953, 1980; Teaford 1985) nor the competing pluralist school (Dahl 1961) grapples with formal groups and institutions at the local level. Only a few pressure groups' scholars have researched the formal organizations that lobby city officials (Zisk et al. 1965; Zisk 1973). Instead, pressure groups' scholars focus their attention on demographic groups (ethnics, WASPs, African Americans, etc.) or economic categories (business people, professionals, teachers, etc.). These scholars analyze how these groups either hold a monopoly on power (for community power structure theorists) or vigorously contest/bargain for it (for pluralists). Even at the local level, groups are not merely the sum of their parts, nor exclusively (or even largely) stand-ins for their affiliated influentials or demographic and economic categories. These modes of analysis are in stark contrast to pressure group studies on the national stage, where intense analysis is conducted of individual organizations and why they become successful, including how they navigate the treacherous waters of effectively lobbying decision-makers while maintaining some semblance of popular legitimacy (*see, e.g.*, Patterson and Singer 2007). Depending on their orientation within the approach, pressure groups theorists maintain that whether Black interests are served is the result either of the whims of power structure or of a pluralistic bargaining process.

Given the relative inattention that each of these major frameworks pays to LPOs—much less to Black LPOs—one might be forgiven for asserting that these organizations serve no meaningful function in urban political ecosystems. Indeed, while a bountiful literature exists on the topic of African American mayors and mayoral campaigns (Burgess 1961; Banfield 1965; Weinberg 1968; Poinsett 1970; Davidson 1972; Nelson and Meranto 1977; Woody 1982; Browning et al. 1984, 1990, 2003; Kleppner 1985; Jennings and King 1986; Payne and Ratzan 1986; Pinderhughes 1987; Alkalimat and Gills 1989; Rich 1989; Stone 1989; Sonenshein 1993; Pohlmann and Kirby 1996; Keiser 1997; Wright 2000; Colburn and Adler 2001; Lane 2001; Moore 2002; Perry 2003; Thompson 2006; Liu and Vanderleeuw 2007; Arrington 2008), very little has been written on purely local political organizations. The author was unable to identify a single book-length study on the activities of these organizations or their role in local political systems. Instead, the locus of scholarly scrutiny has remained firmly in the individual realm of mayors and their campaigns or analyses of the political aspirations of amorphous demographic groups.

Although no book-length work exists, LPOs are not wholly missing from the literature. Banfield and Wilson (1967) noted that these bodies were formed in many large, non-partisan cities to fill the roles previously played by political parties. They stressed that these organizations were among the most powerful local actors, whose endorsements could make or break campaigns. Adrian (1959) contended that slating groups were nothing like political parties, because members of the slate ostensibly lacked any responsibility to the slate as a whole and no influence was wielded on policy after the election.[2] With their study of four Texas cities, Davidson and Fraga (1988) rebutted these contentions, showing that slating groups were normally long-lasting and partly membership-based, exercised influence on policy after the election, and deserved to be regarded as political parties when active in the non-partisan setting. Moreover, they found that these groups often greatly disadvantaged African Americans, Latinos, and poorer Whites, both in the slates they assembled and the policies they advocated. Bridges's (1997) account of municipal reform in southwestern cities provides perhaps the most detailed account of the role LPOs played in local politics. She maintains that LPOs were absolutely vital in the move to "reform" governance in the cities that she studied and that the slates they assembled won overwhelming margins over decades of elections.

Black LPOs are even less visible in the scholarly literature. Some have written at length on locally based civil rights organizations active during the freedom movement of the 1960s, but these organizations usually focused exclusively on direct action, litigation, and lobbying efforts as opposed to electoral politics (Theoharis and Woodard 2003, 2005). Jennings (1992) devoted a book to a "new form" of Black activism that he saw emerging in America that was most noticeable at the local level. However, the defining trait of this "new" activism was its frustration with the managerialism of Black political elites. Making managerialism responsive to Black communities is precisely the task performed by many Black LPOs and worthy of consideration.

Hadley (1987) discusses the emergence of a host of Black LPOs in Louisiana and the role of ministers in forming and sustaining these organizations while Brown and Hartfield (2005) discuss two church-based LPOs in Detroit, the Black Slate and the Fannie Lou Hamer PAC. Brown and Hartfield's chapter provides one of the clearest descriptions of the work Black LPOs engage in, but it argues that the influence of the two groups it studies is primarily due to their connection with the Black church. Given the Black church's historic importance as the largest and wealthiest institution controlled by African Americans, this is sensible. However, in most other cities Black LPOs are *not* directly connected with the church, although they frequently count ministers among their leaders or membership. This observation thus leaves many questions unanswered.

This constitutes the entirety of the literature devoted exclusively to Black LPOs. On the basis of this slim bibliography, one might be tempted to argue that Black LPOs are ancillary to a serious study of urban politics. But this argument is challenged by the frequent references to Black LPOs and their role in works primarily about something else, where scholars invariably mention, if only in passing, that a Black LPO proved important in articulating community demands, lobbying or protesting for specific policies, mobilizing the Black vote, and uniting Black voters behind a slate of candidates believed to be favorable to the community's interests. For example, a strong Black political organization that managed to elect African Americans to the city council and influence policy existed in "Crescent City," the mid-sized southern city which Burgess studied in 1961. Atlanta—now regarded as the pinnacle of African American political empowerment—owes a great deal to its Negro Voters League (NVL), founded in 1948 and influential into the late 1960s. Its sophisticated endorsement strategy, coupled with its ability to guide Black voters, allowed African Americans to hold the balance of power in city elections two decades before they constituted a majority of the population. Atlanta's much-heralded reputation as the "city too busy to hate" during the 1950s and 1960s is attributable to the influence of the League (Bacote 1955; Walker 1963; Banfield 1965; Stone 1989; Bayor 1996; Keiser 1997). Similarly, in Houston, the Harris County Council of Organizations achieved greater responsiveness in local policy by influencing the votes of upward of 70 percent of Black voters (Davidson 1972).

African American politicians and communities across the country swept to power through the hard work of Black LPOs. A partial listing of prominent figures who owe some debt to the efforts of a Black LPO includes: Carl Stokes to Cleveland's Twenty-First District Caucus (Nelson and Meranto 1977; Nelson 1982; Moore 2002); Richard Hatcher to Gary's Muigwithania (Poinsett 1970; Nelson and Meranto 1977; Lane 2001); Harold Washington to Chicago's Task Force for Black Political Empowerment (Alkalimat and Gills 1989); Tom Bradley to Los Angeles's Democratic Minority Conference (Banfield 1965; Sonenshein 1993); Mel King to Boston's Black Political Task Force (Jennings and King 1986); Kenneth Gibson to the Newark United Brothers Organization of Amiri Baraka (Woody 1982; Woodard 1999); Richard Arrington of Birmingham to the Jefferson County Citizens Coalition that he helped to form (Perry 2003; Arrington 2008; Gillespie and Tolbert 2010); and a succession of Black mayors in New Orleans to these kinds of organizations (Schexnider 1982; Perry 1990, 2003; Liu and Vanderleeuw 2007).

It is clear, then, that a gap exists in the urban politics literature. LPOs are frequently acknowledged but substantively ignored, with these organizations too often treated as stand-ins for elites, or as always demonstrating uniform, "cookie-cutter" behavior. Quite unintentionally, structuring accounts of local Black politics in this way serves, in effect, to deny or downplay the collective agency of Black communities.

Black Political Efficacy in Local Politics

This article seeks to take the first steps in asserting the importance of LPOs and its corollary, Black collective agency, in urban politics. In order to do so, a theoretical argument on the relationship between Black LPOs and Black political efficacy is offered here. First, it is argued that, in achieving political efficacy for African Americans at the local level, formal institutions matter. This is because local politics is not best understood through individualistic approaches or by treating local groups as impotent and irrelevant stand-ins for elites or generic bodies. Local groups should be recognized as potentially powerful living organisms that possess sometimes emotional connections with their constituencies and circumstance-specific motives, behaviors, and internal politics. In other words, "collective agency" is just as important—if not more so—than the deeds of individual political actors. The absence of a formal Black LPO would thus impair a city's African American community from achieving maximal empowerment. Secondly, it is argued that *certain types of organizations and activities are more effective than others at achieving empowerment for African Americans at the local level*. In particular, this article argues for a theoretical construct, referred to as "institutionalization," whose contentions are as follows:

1. Formal organizations/institutions that marshal their resources for multiple tactics and seek to impact electoral contests—not those exclusively dedicated to lobbying the victors of those contests or bringing legal challenge to their decisions, or personal campaign committees—matter *most*.
2. African American communities are better served when strong, long-lasting, independent organizations/institutions oriented toward "Black interests" and the "Black community" exist, rather than by *exclusive* use of "alliance," "coalition," or "dependent" organizational models.

It is appropriate to refer to this construct as "institutionalization" because this is the term used by the eminent scholar Mack Jones to describe the early 1970s, a period when African Americans devoted substantial energy to creating independent political and research organizations (Jones 2001).

The contention that *exclusive* use by African Americans of coalition-based organizational strategies is ill-advised is perhaps controversial. Debate over "coalitions" versus "independent power politics" has been a recurring feature of Black politics (Carmichael and Hamilton 1967; Holloway 1968; Sonenshein 1993). It is *not* argued here that coalitions and alliances are undesirable or unimportant for Black interests. In many cases, coalitions are not just demographically inevitable but patently desirable. They frequently result in the promotion of Black interests (Browning et al. 1984, 2003). We should recognize, as Carmichael and Hamilton did in their much-misunderstood theory of Black Power, that alliances inherently include multiple (and often competing) interests. Coalitions thus cannot press for all of the interests of all of their members equally. Some groups within the alliance may routinely be called on to sacrifice their own particular interests "for the good of the coalition," and thus never achieve their goals for entering into coalition in the first place. Groups that are less unified, less powerful, lacking in capacity, or occupy a subordinate position in society are more likely to see their agendas perpetually minimized. If coalition is the exclusive organizing model used by these groups, they are doomed to perpetual dissatisfaction. To win their own demands—and not just be cogs in a machine that produces gains for others—Carmichael and Hamilton recommended that Blacks build strong organizations of their own (Carmichael and Hamilton 1967). Ronald Walters articulates a similar theoretical concept in his study of Black presidential politics. Walters argues that Black political progress has been impeded in the post-civil rights era because African Americans organize almost exclusively within the Democratic Party. This provides only "dependent leverage," which relies on the willingness of the party apparatus to make concessions. Gains are won when Blacks find themselves a part of the "winning team," but since the primary goal of that team is *not* to produce gains for African Americans the potential for progress is inherently limited. More productive, he maintains, is "independent leverage," where African Americans possess power *outside* of any party and where the primary loyalty is not to any party (or alliance) but to Black interests themselves (Walters 1988).

Although the work of Carmichael, Hamilton, and Walters provides a theoretical base for the construct of institutionalization offered here, the latter differs from the former in asserting the importance of *formal, impersonal, long-lasting* organizations and institutions. Earlier authors did not view ad hoc, temporary, informal, or individualistic (e.g., candidate campaign committees) groupings as problematic, provided they achieved gains during their life-spans and were vigorous in their advocacy. Walters, for example, heralds Jesse Jackson's 1984 campaign as a model. Important as that effort was, it was inherently time-constrained, ephemeral, and individualistic in a way that the groups envisioned here are not. Since pressure groups' theories inform us that formal organizations designed to be active in the longer term are essential to the political process, they maximize the efficacy and responsiveness to Black interests called for by "Black Power" and "independent leverage" theories.

In using this theoretical base, the author is fully cognizant of the fact that there exists a debate over what "Black interests" are, or whether "Black interests" and the "Black community" exist at all. Only if one accepts a nakedly simplistic individualism wherein African Americans have nothing in common with one another would organizations articulating Black interests be unnecessary. Although such people do exist and feel that their interests are best responded to by the thousands of other existing pressure groups, they are a minority of a Black community in which a sense of shared fate operationalized in a Black utility heuristic (or, more simply, in *Blackness*) is highly salient (Dawson 1994). Given the pervasiveness of the Black utility heuristic—and the fact that many Black communities across the country *have* succeeded in defining "Black agendas" and rallying Black voters to those agendas (Jennings and King 1986; Alkalimat and Gills 1989; Moore 2002)—defining "Black interests" is not an impossible task.

Assessing Black Political Efficacy and Organizational Efficacy

The theoretical framework outlined above can be restated thusly:

Local Black communities achieve higher levels of political efficacy through the creation and maintenance of institutionalized Black LPOs than they do through the absence of such organizations. As these LPOs increase in strength and organizational efficacy, community-wide Black political efficacy rises as well.

This argument places great value on the notion of "efficacy," necessitating the operationalization of this concept, in two different contexts: Black political efficacy (that is, for the Black community as a whole) and organizational efficacy (that is, for a specific Black LPO). In both contexts that are of interest here, efficacy is defined as the power of a group to collectively shape political events and outcomes, including securing election victories for the candidates of the group's choice and the satisfaction of policy demands made on the system. While the definition for efficacy remains the same in both contexts, to conflate Black political efficacy and organizational efficacy would be a grave mistake. After all, it is possible (though contrary to the argument made above) that a city's Black community could be highly politically efficacious without an organization leading the way. By contrast, it might also be possible for a highly efficacious Black LPO to exist, in terms of securing its own program, but fail to deliver gains for the broader Black community. Although the standards for evaluating Black political efficacy and organizational efficacy must be similar, they must be evaluated separately.

In order to operationalize Black political efficacy at the local level, a Black Political Efficacy Index (BPEI) was created. This index is intended only for use in local political contexts, ranges from 0 (Very Low) to 60 (Very High), and is comprised of six components, each of which has multiple potential ordinal level data values (which are, in turn, linked to specific qualitative thresholds): symbolic representation among elected officials, symbolic representation in public employment, legitimation by elites, the ability to elect a candidate of the Black community's choice, responsiveness to Black policy demands (weighted most heavily within the index), and self-determination/autonomy. The "Very High" designation is reserved for those communities achieving the maximum index score of 60 and is considered an "ideal type." It is readily conceded that component five, policy responsiveness, requires that we acknowledge the existence of "Black interests." This is in keeping with the argument for such interests briefly made above. However, the BPEI does not endogenously define what those interests are and they will likely vary from city to city. Following Walters (2007), Black interests constitute what a majority of African Americans say they are. Adopting this position recognizes the Black community's agency to determine its own interests and agenda, without stifling the significant intra-community dissent that will always exist. A general sense of majority opinion within the African American community can be gleaned from news accounts (particularly in the Black press), other primary sources, and personal interviews.

To operationalize the organizational efficacy of Black LPOs, an Organizational Efficacy Index (OEI) was created. Like the BPEI, the OEI also ranges from 0 (Very Low) to 60 (Very High). The designation of "Very High" is reserved for organizations achieving the maximum index score of 60 and is considered an "ideal type." The OEI is constituted of only four components, each of which has multiple potential ordinal level data values (which are, in turn, linked to specific qualitative thresholds): legitimation by elites, the ability to elect a candidate of its choice in predominantly Black districts, the ability to elect a candidate of its choice in at-large elections, and responsiveness to the organization's policy demands. Although the BPEI is intended to measure the extent to which African American communities are efficacious at transforming the collective agency they inherently possess into securing their tangible political goals—independent of the agenda of any particular LPO—as a practical matter, the agendas of highly efficacious Black LPOs exist in a feedback loop with their constituencies that may render the distinction between the two indices minimal.

Testing the Theory: A Case Study of Kansas City, Missouri, and Freedom, Inc.

In order to test the theory outlined above, the two efficacy indices were employed in a case study of Freedom, Inc., the dominant African American LPO in Kansas City, Missouri. The limitations of the present project do not allow for a full restatement of the case study of Freedom, with its detailed recounting of that organization's history and influence. Instead, the purpose here is to use the broad findings of that case study to evaluate the theoretical argument being advanced. The case study used three methodologies to arrive at its findings: (1) a historiographical approach relying on an exhaustive review of primary source documents and contemporary news accounts from *The Kansas City Star, The Kansas City Times,* and *The Call*, among other media outlets; (2) participant observation on the part of the researcher, who has been involved in Kansas City municipal politics for more than a decade; and (3) a set of twenty detailed, semi-structured interviews with informants knowledgeable about Freedom and Kansas City politics. The highly social, interpersonal, dynamic, and interactive culture of Freedom, Inc. made the sorts of qualitative research employed by the case study more appropriate. Freedom and Kansas City are selected for investigation for two reasons. First, Freedom is the oldest still-existing Black LPO in the country. Sufficient material thus exists to launch a comprehensive investigation, and the organization's longevity strongly implies that it has done *something* right that should be of note to political science scholars. Second, Kansas City is, in many respects, the "average" large American city. In its demographic composition, economic base, geography, and political history, it is a median case. Urban scholars have called it the "most American" and average of cities for this reason. Indeed, *Business Week* magazine once wrote of Kansas City: "It is very average, very typical, very much a composite of every big city in the country" (quoted in Coleman 2006). This averageness implies that any lessons to be gleaned from a case study of Freedom will possess greater portability to other political systems and contexts.

Since its founding in 1962 by seven grassroots leaders, Freedom has become the dominant Black political organization in Kansas City, Missouri. It is the oldest still-existing Black local political organization in the nation (Hart 2006). Its emergence fundamentally shifted the political calculus in the city by creating an independent vehicle for the development of Black political power and the pressing of Black interests. White elites—and no small number of African American residents and politicos—were shocked at Freedom's ability to unify the Black community, to win elections, and to use this newfound power to secure the advancement of Black interests. As political cartoonist Lee Judge put it, when White elites told African American Kansas Citizens to put their faith in the political process, "we didn't expect you to be so good at it" (quoted in Hart 2006). Freedom's multitude of successes include: electing the first African American member to the City Council, beating segregationists at the ballot box to pass a public accommodations ordinance, responding to a violent 1968 urban rebellion, salvaging a fair housing ordinance, eradicating the influence of the machine/factional "plantation bosses," gradually expanding Black symbolic representation on the City Council and in municipal managerial posts, proving an essential part of seven mayoral victories, forcing White elites to treat the Black community with respect in political matters, and (to a degree that varied over the years) politically uniting the Black community. Freedom's other notable successes include the expenditure of additional resources on neighborhood development in the urban core, and the election of Emanuel Cleaver as the city's first African American mayor. Although Freedom had notable defeats—including the defeat of the first Black candidate for mayor (Freedom founder Bruce Watkins, in 1979) and the damage done by a decade of corruption scandals beginning in the mid-1980s—and saw its influence wane, there can be no doubt that Freedom served for decades as the embodiment of the Kansas City Black community's collective agency and as its preeminent voice. In predominantly Black precincts, the Freedom Ballot is not quite the gold standard it once was and younger people often regard the organization as irrelevant or the domain of an older generation whose service is appreciated but whose time has passed. Even with these challenges, majorities of voters in the "Freedom Wards"—the wards that have historically been predominantly Black—still cast their votes for Freedom, Inc.'s slate and its endorsement is sought by nearly all candidates for public office.

Freedom is more than simply a "non-partisan slating group" although its influence is definitely felt through the issuance of the black-and-gold "Freedom Ballot"; it is also a pressure group, a protest organization (though protest has waned as one of its tools), a civil rights movement, a space for the development of a local Black agenda, and the political voice of a largely united Black community. It is no overstatement to say that, aside from the Black Church, Freedom, Inc. has been more meaningful and important for Kansas City's African American community than any other local institution. Freedom, Inc.'s impact has been revolutionary, a fact reflected in the esteem in which the organization continues to be held by many African American Kansas citizens. As one former elected official put it in an interview, "I would hate to think what life in Kansas City would have been like, certainly in the '60s and '70s and even early '80s, had Freedom not been around" (Interview).

The sentiment expressed by this interview subject—and the theory argued for above—are borne out by an analysis of Kansas City's BPEI and OEI results. These two indices were used to "rate" the organizational efficacy of Freedom and the political efficacy of Kansas City's African American community at various intervals from 1962 to 2007, based on a qualitative analysis conducted through the methodologies described above. These ratings are intended to give readers a general sense of where the LPO and the broader African American community are at a particular moment in time as well as to allow us to track how efficacy changes over time; they are not intended to be exhaustive or to be interpreted without the benefit of substantiating detail.

Figure 1 presents a graphic rendering of change in Freedom's OEI scores and Kansas City's BPEI scores between 1962 and 2007. As can be seen from this graph, when Freedom was founded in 1962, Kansas City's African American community was deeply inefficacious. African American residents had almost no political power, with few representatives of even the symbolic variety, no ability to influence public policy, and little control over their own political destinies. As might be expected, Freedom was not terribly efficacious at its founding, when it was but one of many political organizations "serving" the Black community and when it was attempting to end the stranglehold of the old-line, machine-oriented Democratic factions, which operated in Black wards but were White-led and -staffed. Through a confluence of circumstance, personality, and smart politics, the organization rapidly took off, expanding beyond its original base in

Figure 1.
Freedom, Inc.'s Organization Efficacy Index (OEI) Scores and Kansas City's
Black Political Efficacy Index (BPEI) Scores, 1962–2007

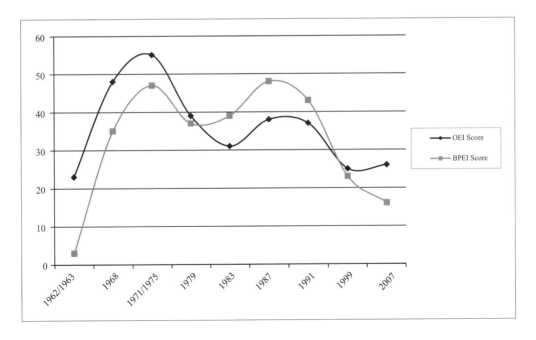

the city's nearly all-Black fourteenth ward and becoming an important actor in local politics. The organization became fully institutionalized by the early 1970s and its ascent in power and efficacy in local politics continued until 1979, when Bruce Watkins's loss in the mayoral race and its effects proved devastating to Freedom. This decline persisted through most of the 1980s—when Freedom was buffeted by the refusal of some clergy to support its political leadership, its withdrawal from the municipal policy making process, and increasingly common claims of corruption and cliquishness within its ranks—before a canny political strategy in the 1987 mayoral election resuscitated the organization's reputation and modestly improved its efficacy.[3] Freedom achieved its greatest municipal triumph when it assisted in electing Emanuel Cleaver mayor in 1991 despite the fact that the organization's efficacy was lower than it had been during the previous attempt at electing an African American mayor. Paradoxically, the election of an African American mayor did not contribute to enhanced efficacy for Freedom but rather detracted from it, as the organization's historic role as the intermediary between White elites and the Black community was unconsciously usurped by Cleaver. Freedom's organizational efficacy steadily declined after 1991 and the organization gradually lost the attributes demanded by the construct of institutionalization. These findings are entirely consistent with the views of interview subjects, who invariably described Freedom's "glory days" as being in the 1970s and the period from the mid-1990s onward as one of decay.

As Figure 1 demonstrates, Kansas City's Black community followed a similar trajectory in its political efficacy. Before the founding of Freedom, the community hovered near absolute inefficacy, with no meaningful voice in elections or policy making and minimal symbolic representation. Within a few years of Freedom's founding, the Black community became reasonably efficacious, able to claim victories like a public accommodations ordinance, fair housing ordinance, Model Cities spending, and the appointment of several African American department directors. In the 1980s, the community experienced much higher efficacy than Freedom did, but still generally followed the pattern set by the LPO. The high level of political efficacy attained by the African American community during the 1980s is directly attributable to the considerable power wielded by several Black and Latino members of the City Council—all powerbrokers within Freedom, who owed their district-based seats to Freedom's support—who managed to "run things at City Hall" even in the absence of holding formal positions of power (e.g., committee chairs). Quite contrary to the predictions of those who championed his election, Emanuel Cleaver's mayoralty did not usher in an era of unprecedented advancement of Black interests. Although Cleaver's administration had some notable achievements for Black residents (such as the redevelopment of the city's historic Jazz District, in the heart of the city's African American community), Black political efficacy fell over the course of his two terms and was considerably *higher* during the 1970s than at *any* point in the Cleaver years. The Cleaver years were a virtual paradise compared to what followed, when Black political efficacy plummeted to its lowest level since the 1960s and even symbolic action on Black interests was rarely taken.

There is thus ample evidence to support the theory that the organizational efficacy of Black LPOs, institutionalization, and Black political efficacy are firmly linked. As Freedom, Inc. became more institutionalized, its organizational efficacy increased; as Freedom's organizational efficacy increased, the Black community's political efficacy also rose.

Declines in Freedom's efficacy were accompanied by similar falls in the efficacy of the broader African American community. This relationship was not absolute. Organizational success by Freedom usually preceded policy victories by the broader community, while the community managed to maintain some efficacy even during the dark days of the early 1980s. Even then, a relationship between the two variables existed. For example, the Black community's ability to extract policy concessions during the 1980s is attributable to the seniority accrued by elected officials who relied on Freedom's support to return to office term after term. In other words, *in the pursuit of African American interests in local government, the existence of a strong Black political organization vocalizing and mobilizing support for those interests mattered a great deal.*

However, it should be stressed that linking institutionalization, organizational efficacy, and political efficacy together is not a comprehensive theory. More needs to be said—or, rather, learned—about the conditions under which LPOs become strong and efficacious.

Implications of the Findings

In short, the findings reported above provide initial, tentative support to the theoretical framework presented above and to the proposition, continually reasserted throughout this paper, that LPOs are a vital component of the urban political ecosystem. Beyond the support provided to these arguments, though, there are two major implications of these findings. The first, and most important, is that African American communities see their interests—however one chooses to define those interests—best served when strong, institutionalized organizations exist to advocate for them. As the decline in Black political efficacy during Emanuel Cleaver's mayoralty in Kansas City demonstrated, it is not enough for African American communities to have even sympathetic "Black faces in high places." In order to produce concrete benefits for Black communities, strong organizations must exist which are single-mindedly devoted to the pursuit of Black interests. These organizations should pursue multiple objectives, should be involved in the policy-making process, and should possess the political clout to strike terror in the hearts of elected officials by genuinely holding them accountable at the ballot box.

The research presented here, admittedly limited in scope as it is to a single large city and a single Black LPO, implies that urban Black communities that feel neglected, disenfranchised, or actively harmed by their municipal leadership possess the agency and ability to transform those conditions. This research implies that the *best* route to transforming these conditions lies not in the traditional fixation on electing a Black mayor or City Council majority. Instead, the Kansas City experience suggests that local African American communities would be better served by building standing, permanent political organizations that are not beholden to any one particular individual or faction and which can serve as the unified political voice of the community. These organizations should be open, transparent, democratic, accountable, possessed of unchallenged integrity, dynamic, responsive to urgent community needs, deeply connected to the grassroots, independent, and organized, using a "Black interests" or "independent leverage" model. Doing so will grant the African American community the leverage and clout that it requires in order to successfully press its demands on the system, gain political empowerment, and achieve high levels of political efficacy.

In order for this area of research to be most useful, more must be learned about *how* Black LPOs go about their work and achieve organizational efficacy. A number of variables were identified above that led to Freedom's success and several others were identified that were harmful to the LPO's work. It is readily acknowledged that it is far easier to identify these characteristics in an academic environment than it is to practice them in the hard-scrabble world of politics. Still, it is hoped that the implications of these findings—particularly the ones related to a mass orientation versus a professionalized one and the need for a democratic and inclusive political culture—can be used by Black LPOs to guide them in their quests for African American liberation, equality, and justice.

Similar research should be performed in other cities and on other Black LPOs to determine whether the Kansas City experience is an anomaly. Regardless, it is hoped that this research can be a starting point for a discussion about the best way to advance African American interests in the twenty-first century. As scholars within the discipline of Black politics like Jones (2008), Smith (1996), and Walters (2005) have argued, the past three decades have not been kind to African Americans at either the local or federal levels. This research's findings suggest that this dearth of progress is in part attributable to the fact that Black politics at the national level and in many localities has *not* been institutionalized and that strong Black LPOs and national political organizations do not exist. The research's findings suggest that the best way to advance African American interests in the twenty-first century—at least in urban politics—is by concentrating energies on institutionalizing Black politics and building efficacious Black political organizations.

Notes

1. These organizations are sometimes called "slating groups," "non-partisan slating groups," or "political clubs" by other scholars. The term "local political organization" is used by this author to refer to these entities because it is inclusive of the wide range of activities they may undertake (extending far beyond assembling "slates"), is appropriate in both partisan and non-partisan electoral systems, and better conveys the long-lasting nature of these groups. The term also implies a higher level of structural complexity and the presence of a distinct organizational culture, both of which are to be found in the groups being described here.
2. Even the contention that members lacked any responsibility to the slate is of dubious veracity. Candidates selected for a slate almost always were asked—and often required—to contribute funds to advance the *entire* slate, and to appear at functions endorsing the entire slate. For many years, Kansas City's Citizens Association imposed a notorious "loyalty oath" that required slate members to support the *entire* slate. Supporting the entire slate meant refraining from donating funds to other slates on which they might appear, if the competing slate featured any candidates not endorsed by the Citizens Association.
3. It bears noting that Freedom's efficacy at other levels of government was growing at the same time, with the LPO succeeding at electing Alan Wheat as Kansas City's first Black congressman.

References

Adrian, Charles R. 1959. "A Typology for Nonpartisan Elections." *Western Political Quarterly* 12: 449–58.

Alkalimat, Abdul, and Doug Gills. 1989. *Harold Washington and the Crisis of Black Power in Chicago.* Chicago, IL: Twenty-First Century Books and Publications.

Arrington, Richard. 2008. *There's Hope for the World: The Memoir of Birmingham, Alabama's First African American Mayor.* Tuscaloosa, AL: University of Alabama Press.

Bacote, C. A. 1955. "The Negro in Atlanta Politics." *Phylon* 16, no. 4: 335–50.

Banfield, Edward C. 1965. *Big City Politics: A Comparative Guide to the Political Systems of Atlanta, Boston, Detroit, El Paso, Los Angeles, Miami, St. Louis, and Seattle.* New York: Random House.

Banfield, Edward C., and James Q. Wilson. 1967. *City Politics.* Cambridge, MA: Harvard University Press.

Bent, Devin. 1982. "Partisan Elections and Public Policy: Response to Black Demands in Large American Cities." *Journal of Black Studies* 12, no. 3: 291–314.

Bobo, Lawrence, and Franklin D. Gilliam, Jr. 1990. "Race, Sociopolitical Participation, and Empowerment." *The American Political Science Review* 84, no. 2: 377–93.

Bridges, Amy. 1997. *Morning Glories: Municipal Reform in the Southwest*. Princeton, NJ: Princeton University Press.

Brown, Ronald E., and Carolyn Hartfield. 2005. "Black Churches and the Formation of Political Action Committees in Detroit." In *Black Churches and Local Politics: Clergy Influence, Organizational Partnerships, and Civic Empowerment*, ed. R. Drew Smith and Fredrick C. Harris, 151–70. Lanham, MD: Rowman and Littlefield.

Browning, Rufus P., Dale Rogers Marshall, and David H. Tabb. 1984. *Protest Is Not Enough: The Struggle of Blacks and Hispanics for Equality in Urban Politics*. Berkeley, CA: University of California Press.

———. 1990. *Racial Politics in American Cities*. New York: Longman.

———. 2003. *Racial Politics in American Cities*, 3rd edn. New York: Longman.

Burgess, M. Elaine. 1961. *Negro Leadership in a Southern City*. New Haven, CT: College and University Press.

Carmichael, Stokely, and Charles V. Hamilton. 1967. *Black Power: The Politics of Liberation in America*. New York: Vintage Books.

Colburn, David R., and Jeffrey S. Adler. 2001. *African-American Mayors: Race, Politics, and the American City*. Urbana, IL: University of Illinois Press.

Coleman, Richard P. 2006. *The Kansas City Establishment: Leadership Through Two Centuries in a Midwestern Metropolis*. Manhattan, NY: KS Publishing.

Dahl, Robert A. 1961. *Who Governs? Democracy and Power in an American City*. New Haven, CT: Yale University Press.

Davidson, Chandler, and Luis Ricardo Fraga. 1988. "Slating Groups as Parties in a 'Nonpartisan' Setting." *Western Political Quarterly* 41, no. 2: 373–90.

Davidson, Chandler. 1972. *Biracial Politics: Conflict and Coalition in the Metropolitan South*. Baton Rouge, LA: Louisiana State University Press.

Dawson, Michael C. 1994. *Behind the Mule: Race and Class in African-American Politics*. Princeton, NJ: Princeton University Press.

Gillespie, Andra, and Emma Tolbert. 2010. "Racial Authenticity and Redistricting: A Comparison of Artur Davis's 2000 and 2002 Congressional Campaigns." In *Whose Black Politics? Cases in Post-Racial Black Leadership*, ed. Andra Gillespie, 45–66. New York: Routledge.

Hadley, Charles D. 1987. "The Transformation of the Role of Black Ministers and Black Political Organizations in Louisiana Politics." In *Blacks and Southern Politics*, ed. Laurence W. Moreland, Robert P. Steed, and Tod A. Baker, 133–48. New York: Praeger.

Hajnal, Zoltan L. 2001. "White Residents, Black Incumbents, and a Declining Racial Divide." *The American Political Science Review* 95, no. 3: 603–17.

Hart, Amy. 2006. *The Founding of Freedom: A Kansas City Civil Rights Organization since 1962*. Master's thesis, Central Missouri State University.

Holloway, Harry. 1968. "Negro Political Strategy: Coalition or Independent Power Politics." *Social Science Quarterly* 49: 534–47.

Hunter, Floyd. 1980. *Community Power Succession: Atlanta's Policy-Makers Revisited*. Chapel Hill, NC: University of North Carolina Press.

Hunter, Floyd. 1953. *Community Power Structure: A Study of Decision Makers*. Chapel Hill, NC: University of North Carolina Press.

Jennings, James, and Mel King. 1986. *From Access to Power: Black Politics in Boston*. Cambridge, MA: Schenkman Books.

Jennings, James. 1992. *The Politics of Black Empowerment: The Transformation of Black Activism in Urban America*. Detroit, MI: Wayne State University Press.

Jones, Mack H. 2001. "Politics and Organizational Options: Comments on Essay VI: 'The Next Five Years: II. Organizational Options." *National Political Science Review* 8: 50–57.

Jones, Ricky L. 2008. *What's Wrong with Obamamania?: Black America, Black Leadership, and the Death of Political Imagination*. Albany, NY: State University of New York Press.

Kaufmann, Karen M. 2003. "Black and Latino Voters in Denver: Responses to Each Other's Political Leadership." *Political Science Quarterly* 118, no. 1: 107–25.

———. 2004. *The Urban Voter: Group Conflict & Mayoral Voting Behavior in American Cities*. Ann Arbor, MI: University of Michigan Press.

Keiser, Richard A. 1997. *Subordination or Empowerment? African-American Leadership and the Struggle for Urban Political Power*. New York: Oxford University Press.

Keiser, Richard A., and Katherine Underwood. 2000. *Minority Politics at the Millennium*. New York: Garland Publishing.

Kleppner, Paul. 1985. *Chicago Divided: The Making of a Black Mayor*. DeKalb, IL: Northern Illinois University Press.

Lane, James B. 2001. "Black Political Power and Its Limits: Gary Mayor Richard G. Hatcher's Administration, 1968–87." In *African-American Mayors: Race, Politics, and the American City*, ed. David R. Colburn and Jeffrey S. Adler, 57–79. Urbana, IL: University of Illinois Press.

Liu, Baodong, and James M. Vanderleeuw. 2007. *Race Rules: Electoral Politics in New Orleans, 1965–2006*. Lanham, MD: Lexington Books.

Mladenka, Kenneth R. 1989. "Blacks and Hispanics in Urban Politics." *The American Political Science Review* 83, no. 1: 165–91.

Molotch, Harvey. 1976. "The City as Growth Machine." *American Journal of Sociology* 82: 309–32.

Moore, Leonard N. 2002. *Carl B. Stokes and the Rise of Black Political Power*. Urbana, IL: University of Illinois Press.

Nelson, William E., Jr. 1982. "Cleveland: The Rise and Fall of the New Black Politics." In *The New Black Politics: The Search for Political Power*, ed. Michael B. Preston and Lenneal J. Henderson, 187–208. New York: Longman.

Nelson, William E., Jr., and Philip J. Meranto. 1977. *Electing Black Mayors: Political Action in the Black Community*. Columbus, OH: Ohio State University Press.

Patterson, Kelly D., and Matthew M. Singer. 2007. "Targeting Success: The Enduring Power of the NRA." In *Interest Group Politics,* 7th edn., ed. Allan J. Cigler and Burdett A. Loomis, 37–64. Washington, DC: CQ Press.

Payne, J. Gregory, and Scott C. Ratzan. 1986. *Tom Bradley, The Impossible Dream: A Biography*. Santa Monica, CA: Roundtable Publishing.

Perry, Huey L. 1990. "The Evolution and Impact of Biracial Coalitions and Black Mayors in Birmingham and New Orleans." In *Racial Politics in American Cities*, ed. Rufus P. Browning, Dale Rogers Marshall, and David H. Tabb, 140–52. New York: Longman.

———. 2003. "The Evolution and Impact of Biracial Coalitions and Black Mayors in Birmingham and New Orleans." In *Racial Politics in American Cities*, 3rd edn., ed. Rufus P. Browning, Dale Rogers Marshall, and David H. Tabb, 227–54. New York: Longman.

Pinderhughes, Dianne M. 1987. *Race and Ethnicity in Chicago Politics: A Reexamination of Pluralist Theory*. Urbana, IL: University of Illinois Press.

Pohlmann, Marcus D., and Michael P. Kirby. 1996. *Racial Politics at the Crossroads: Memphis Elects Dr. W.W. Herenton*. Knoxville, TN: University of Tennessee Press.

Poinsett, Alex. 1970. *Black Power, Gary Style: The Making of Mayor Richard Gordon Hatcher*. Chicago, IL: Johnson Publishing Company.

Rich, Wilbur C. 1989. *Coleman Young and Detroit Politics: From Social Activist to Power Broker*. Detroit, MI: Wayne State University Press.

Schexnider, Alvin J. 1982. "Political Mobilization in the South: The Election of a Black Mayor in New Orleans." In *The New Black Politics: The Search for Political Power*, ed. Michael B. Preston, Lenneal J. Henderson Jr., and Paul Puryear, 221–40. New York: Longman.

Smith, Robert C. 1996. *We Have No Leaders: African Americans in the Post-Civil Rights Era*. Albany, NY: State University of New York Press.

Sonenshein, Raphael J. 1993. *Politics in Black and White: Race and Power in Los Angeles*. Princeton, NJ: Princeton University Press.

Stone, Clarence N. 1989. *Regime Politics: Governing Atlanta, 1946–1988*. Lawrence, KS: University of Kansas Press.

Teaford, Jon C. 1985. "New Life for an Old Subject: Investigating the Structure of Urban Rule." *American Quarterly* 37, no. 3: 346–56.

Theoharis, Jeanne, and Komozi Woodard. 2003. *Freedom North: Black Freedom Struggles Outside the South, 1940–1980*. New York: Palgrave Macmillan.

———. 2005. *Groundwork: Local Black Freedom Movements in America*. New York: New York University Press.

Thompson, J. Phillip, III. 2006. *Double Trouble: Black Mayors, Black Communities, and the Call for a Deep Democracy*. New York: Oxford University Press.

Walker, Jack L. 1963. "Protest and Negotiation: A Case Study of Negro Leadership in Atlanta, Georgia." *Midwest Journal of Political Science* 7, no. 2: 99–124.

Walters, Ronald W. 1988. *Black Presidential Politics in America: A Strategic Approach.* Albany, NY: State University of New York Press.

———. 2005. *Freedom Is Not Enough: Black Voters, Black Candidates, and American Presidential Politics.* Lanham, MD: Rowman and Littlefield.

———. 2007. "Barack Obama and the Politics of Blackness." *The Journal of Black Studies* 38, no. 1: 7–29.

Weinberg, Kenneth G. 1968. *Black Victory: Carl Stokes and the Winning of Cleveland.* Chicago, IL: Quadrangle Books.

Woodard, Komozi. 1999. *A Nation within a Nation: Amiri Baraka (LeRoi Jones) and Black Power Politics.* Chapel Hill, NC: University of North Carolina Press.

Woody, Bette. 1982. *Managing Crisis Cities: The New Black Leadership and the Politics of Resource Allocation.* Westport, CT: Greenwood Press.

Wright, Sharon D. 2000. *Race, Power, and Political Emergence in Memphis.* New York: Garland.

Zisk, Betty H. 1973. *Local Interest Politics: A One-Way Street.* Indianapolis, IN: The Bobbs-Merrill Company.

Zisk, Betty H., Heinz Eulau, and Kenneth Prewitt. 1965. "City Councilmen and the Group Struggle: A Typology of Role Orientation." *The Journal of Politics* 27, no. 3: 618–46.

The Effects of Concentrated Poverty on Black and White Political Participation in the Southern Black Belt

Sharon D. Wright Austin*
University of Florida
Sekou M. Franklin
Middle Tennessee State University
Angela K. Lewis
University of Alabama-Birmingham

Introduction

The Black-Belt region of the United States, also referred to as the "cotton counties" or "plantation counties," was defined by Booker T. Washington as "counties where Blacks outnumber Whites" (Washington 1965). Currently, it is characterized as a southern area with a sizable Black population in parts of Virginia, North and South Carolina, Georgia, Florida, Alabama, Mississippi, Louisiana, Texas, Arkansas, and Tennessee (Wimberly et al. 1992, 1993). Historically, high rates of concentrated poverty and social isolation have pervaded Black-Belt counties because of their large populations of disproportionately poor, uneducated, unemployed, and politically powerless residents (Morrison 1987, 210; Falk and Rankin 1992, 300; Swanson et al. 1994; Wimberly 1997).

This study assesses the impact of concentrated poverty on the political views and participation of Black and White residents of Florida, Louisiana, Mississippi, and Texas Black-Belt communities. We examine two questions. First, are poor Whites and Blacks in these communities less likely to engage in voting and non-electoral political activities than individuals in the same communities with a higher socioeconomic status? Second, do poor Whites and Blacks have more pessimistic attitudes toward government than individuals from higher economic groups in the communities where they live? The answers to these questions will provide insight into the political participation of poor Whites and Blacks living in close proximity to each other and experiencing similar conditions of poverty, unemployment, and racial and class stratification. It compares their political attitudes and participation to those of less impoverished Black-Belt residents and therefore adds to a fuller understanding of race, class, and political behavior.

Concentrated Poverty, Social Isolation, and Political Participation

We wish to examine the impact of individual and neighborhood poverty on the political behavior of Whites and African Americans in the southern Black-Belt. Scholarly research finds that the residents of predominantly African American neighborhoods plagued by concentrated poverty rates of 20 percent and above are also disadvantaged by their "social isolation" from the middle class and from institutions like churches, community, social, or religious organizations that encourage political participation. The combination of social isolation and neighborhood poverty severely reduces their opportunities to network with other productive individuals, participate effectively in politics, and influence public policies (Alex-Assensoh 1998, 16; Tigges et al. 1998, 61).

Some analytical studies have examined the negative impact of concentrated poverty and social isolation in urban communities (Wilson 1987; Wacquant and Wilson 1989; Massey and Eggers 1990; Wilson 1991; Massey and Denton 1993; Tigges et al. 1998; Rankin and Quane 2000), but those conditions also impact rural areas. Black and White neighborhoods in the southern Black-Belt counties are ideal for review because of their chronic widespread poverty (Wimberly and Morris 1997, 10). In these communities, poor Whites and Blacks are isolated from the middle class, even if they live in close proximity to middle-class neighborhoods, because of the complex hierarchical class relations there. Individuals from poor and middle-class backgrounds may only live a few neighborhoods apart, but seldom interact with each other (Duncan 1999). They attend separate churches, send their children to separate schools, and fail to establish friendships because of the strict unwritten social mores of their communities.

While poor Whites are socially isolated from wealthier Whites because of their class, African Americans have to grapple with both class and racial polarization. Not only are most African American rural residents either poor or working class, they are also residentially and socially segregated from both poor and middle-class White citizens (Austin 2006). In addition, the problems associated with a lack of educational achievement, job losses, and single female-headed households are just as severe or more so in the rural regions of the southern Black-Belt as they are in urban ones (Wimberly and Morris 1997). A key but inadequately researched question is whether concentrated poverty and social isolation in rural communities also foster political discontent among the poor, both Black and White.

We are studying the political behavior of our respondents because of the importance of political participation in America. By engaging in electoral and non-electoral participation, individuals have the ability to select the officials who govern this country and to demand that they use their positions to address our local, state, and national problems. A large body of literature questions the factors that motivate individuals to vote. Many vote either because they sense it as their civic duty or because they believe their vote will help others (Brady et al. 1995; Fowler 2006). Others participate because they possess resources such as time, money, the ability to mobilize voters, strong interests in political affairs, a desire to influence governmental decisions, and an unyielding trust of the governmental process (Brady et al. 1995, 371). Most of this literature concludes that socioeconomic variables (such as higher educational, income, and occupational statuses) motivate individuals to vote more so than others. For example, older, White, educated, female, married, wealthier, and religious individuals turn out at higher rates than other groups (Verba and Nie 1972; Wolfinger and Rosenstone 1980; Verba et al. 1993; Lijphart

1997, 2–5; Edwards et al. 2008, 290–91). Thus, these findings clearly conclude that persons with lower incomes and persons of color have lower voting participation. We wish to determine the validity of these findings by examining respondents in a region largely populated by poor people and minorities.

In addition, many assumptions have been made about the political efficacy of the poor. Their lower voting participation has been attributed to either a lack of interest in politics or a distrust of government (Shingles 1981; DeLuca 1995). If the poor are apathetic and/or distrustful of the political system, it would naturally follow that their political cynicism would surpass that of more affluent Black-Belt residents. After we examine the political participation of our respondents, we will then assess their attitudes about politics. The two hypotheses in this research follow.

H1: The Black and White residents of neighborhoods plagued by concentrated poverty are less likely to vote, but are more likely to participate in non-electoral activities. We expect the residents of impoverished neighborhoods to have lower voting rates, but to actively engage in alternative political activities. The current literature suggests this hypothesis. As previously mentioned, the poor vote at considerably lower rates than more affluent individuals as a consequence of their lower incomes, educational levels, and inadequate feelings of political efficacy (Scott and Acock 1979, 361; Gaventa 1980, 141). It was once believed that the lower voting participation of the rural poor often resulted from their fears of retaliation from powerful White elites (Salamon and Van Evera 1973). Lately, scholarly research has disputed these findings due to protections provided by laws such as the Voting Rights Act of 1965. Lower voting turnouts in poor communities were subsequently explained by other factors, such as apathy and/or disappointment with the abilities of elected officials to deliver economic benefits to communities (Morrison 1987, 212).

Despite their lower voting participation, we expect the non-electoral participation of poorer neighborhood residents to surpass that of middle-class neighborhood residents. Apathy may suppress the willingness of individuals to vote, but does not suppress other forms of political action. For example, it has been shown that African Americans in rural areas vote less frequently than Whites, but participate in "cooperative" political activities more frequently. These activities involve working collectively in political, religious, and social organizations that address their community's problems (Gaventa 1980, 47, 162; Austin 2006, 156). In many instances, these residents believe they can receive more substantial benefits from political elites through their work in community organizations than through the voting process (Austin 2006, 164–65). Many live in small, poor, predominantly Black towns with majority Black political establishments, but suffer impoverished conditions. Because of the inability of Black politicians to improve their plight, residents engage in activities such as attending community meetings, contacting public officials, signing petitions, and discussing local and national political issues) (Alex-Assensoh 1998, 92). These activities allow them to address their communities' problems despite their lack of financial resources.

Research on urban cities echoes the findings of the lower electoral, but higher non-electoral participation among the Black and White residents of concentrated poverty neighborhoods. A comprehensive study of the impact of concentrated poverty and single parenthood on the political behavior of Black and White residents of inner-city neighborhoods in Columbus, Ohio, finds that Black and White residents of concentrated poverty neighborhoods are less likely to vote than the residents of other low-poverty neighborhoods (Alex-Assensoh 1998, 102). However, their lower voter turnout rates are not indicative of a lack of interest in politics because their participation in some non-electoral political activities surpasses that of Black and White residents of low-poverty neighborhoods (Alex-Assensoh 1998, 93). The impoverished Black residents of extremely poor neighborhoods are more likely to attend community meetings as well as discuss local and national political issues than White middle-class residents of neighborhoods with little poverty (Alex-Assensoh 1998, 92). Also, they are more likely to contact public officials and attend community meetings than middle-class Black residents of neighborhoods with low rates of poverty (Alex-Assensoh 1998, 94). Similarly, the poor White residents of neighborhoods plagued by concentrated poverty are more likely to contact public officials and discuss national political issues than middle-class White residents of neighborhoods that are not poor. These residents also contact their local elected officials more frequently than middle-class Black residents of middle-class neighborhoods (Alex-Assensoh 1998, 92–93). We believe that rural Black-Belt residents also devote their energies to a similarly high rate of non-electoral participation.

H2: Neither Black nor White residents of concentrated poverty neighborhoods have more cynical attitudes about government than individuals residing in higher-income neighborhoods.

Consistent with the findings of Berry et al. (1991), we expect to find little evidence that poor African Americans and Whites have more pessimistic attitudes about the political process than working-class and middle-class Blacks and Whites. Their survey of poor and "nonpoor" Blacks and Whites examines their trust in government, feelings of personal political efficacy, sense of community, and political activities in Birmingham, Dayton, Portland, St. Paul, and San Antonio. More specifically, their survey participants consisted of poor residents of poor neighborhoods, poor residents of nonpoor neighborhoods, nonpoor residents of poor neighborhoods, and nonpoor residents of nonpoor neighborhoods (Berry et al. 1991, 359–60).

Although their study examines political behavior in cities, we expect similar findings in our study of poor rural neighborhood residents because urban and rural community residents often experience similar problems. The political constraints in some of these cities resemble those in rural America because of racially polarized voting patterns, strained class relationships, and other barriers (such as machine politics) which inhibit the ability of the poor to elect their preferred representatives (Perry 2003; Rosales 2000). Other research disputes the fact that the African American residents of poor neighborhoods have pessimistic views about the political process, but nevertheless are less likely to participate (Cohen and Dawson 1993, 298).

The research by Berry et al. concludes that poor African American residents of poor neighborhoods have positive attitudes about the political system that do not significantly differ from those of middle-class Black neighborhood residents. When asked about their "trust in the government" and "sense of community," poor African Americans indicate the same degree of trust and sense of community as nonpoor African Americans. However, poor Black respondents do not believe that they have as much ability to improve their community's plight by working in the political system as their nonpoor counterparts (Berry et al. 1991, 366–69).

Moreover, poor Blacks and poor Whites possess similar attitudes about the political process. Both groups have the same amount of trust in government, but poor Black respondents are more likely to believe that they "do not have much to say in government" and that "government is too complicated" than poor Whites (Berry et al. 1991, 366). In addition, poor Blacks have a stronger sense of community than poor Whites. Berry et al. conclude, "Although race does influence people's sense of their effectiveness, the less positive attitudes of Blacks do not seem to carry over into apathetic behavior" (Berry et al. 1991, 366). Essentially, the attitudes of poor Blacks and Whites about the political process do not significantly differ from those of middle-class Blacks and Whites (Berry et al. 1991, 362).

Data and Methodology

From 2008 to 2011, we interviewed 1,028 residents of rural Florida, Louisiana, Mississippi, and Texas Black-Belt neighborhoods with Black and White poverty rates ranging between 28 and 71 percent (*see* Appendix 1). Appendix 2 provides a demographic profile of our respondents. Poverty has been defined for both the individual (based on household incomes) and neighborhood (based on the percentage of households in a census tract with incomes below the poverty line) (Cohen and Dawson 1993, 288). In this study, the focus is on both. We assess individual poverty on the basis of an individual's income, household type, and number of children.[1] We then define families of four with incomes of $22,000 or less as impoverished; between $22,500 to $60,000 as working class; and with incomes above $60,000 as middle class. Lastly, we distinguish low-poverty neighborhoods (0 to 12.3 percent poverty rates) from moderate (12.4 to 19.9 percent poverty rates) and extreme poverty neighborhoods (rates of 20 percent or more) (Bishaw 2005, 1).

To determine levels of neighborhood poverty, surveys were distributed to residents of neighborhoods within the census tracts in Appendix 1. First, we calculate our sample size based on the "sample size calculator" which allows researchers to determine the sample sizes of the populations under review in their research after determining the confidence level and confidence interval (http://www.surveysystem.com/sscalc.htm).[2] At a 95 percent confidence level, and a confidence interval of +4, we select a sample size of 301 in Florida because of the 701 neighborhood residents in our targeted areas, 201 in Louisiana (301 neighborhood residents), 162 in Mississippi (201 residents), and 364 in Texas (923 residents).

Second, we use a logistic regression methodology to test our hypotheses because it allows us to determine the extent to which our independent variables impact our dependent variables. In the first hypothesis, we wish to assess the impact of the independent variable (concentrated poverty) on voting which we coded as 3 for "always vote," 2 for "sometimes miss one," 1 for "rarely vote," and 0 for "never vote."

In the second part of hypothesis one, which deals with non-electoral activities, we measure their involvement in civic, political, and religious groups as well as their other forms of political participation. In the second hypothesis, we again want to determine the impact of residence in a poor neighborhood, but on an individual's attitudes about politics, rather than his or her political participation. In particular, we wish to examine our respondents' views about both their local and national governments. We examine these views separately because an individual may have pessimistic views about their local governments, but not the national government and vice versa. (For a full version of the survey instrument used in this study, see Appendix 3.)

Findings

Based on the data presented in Table 1, we can confirm the first hypothesis. In the first part of the first hypothesis, we expect the Black and White residents of concentrated poverty neighborhoods to vote less often than Blacks and Whites who reside in working-class and middle-class neighborhoods. We find that both Black and White residents of

Table 1.
Impact of Concentrated Poverty on Voting Participation, Non-Voting Participation, and Political Attitudes of Black-Belt Residents

	Electoral Participation		Non-electoral Participation		Political Attitudes	
	Local	National	Organizational Memberships	Non-electoral Activities	Local Govrn	National Govrn
	B (S.E.)	B (S.E.)	B (S.E.)	B (S.E.)	B (S.E.)	B (S.E.)
Neighborhood Socioeconomic Status:						
Black poverty	−2.9	−1.7	38.4	6.3	−.58	−.18 (.29)
White poverty	−1.8	−.54 (.98)	41.0	17.5	−.54	−.62 (1.53)*
Black	1.5 (.71)*	.28 (.78)*	2.4 (6000.0)	−2.9	−.04	−.60 (.26)
White working/ middle-class	1.76 (.54)*	.38 (.48)	.16 (.21)	−.14 (.23)	−.32 (.21)	−.68 (25)
Control Variables:						
Age	.03 (.58)*	.15 (.58)*	3.6 (1.0)*	19.0	−.62	−.77 (.31)
Income	.23 (.23)*	.34 (.28)*	.28 (.26)	1.0 (.54)**	−.17	1.2 (.79)
Education	3.6 (.59)*	2.6	−17.2	5.7 (1.4)*	−.70	−.47 (.47)
Gender	−2.9 (.55)	−3.8 (.60)	57.6	41.7	−.95	−1.39 (.49)
Marital Status	1.1 (.38)*	1.8 (.37)*	−.41 (.41)	2.7 (1.1)*	−.56 (.66)	.82 (.69)
Constant	−.61	1.11 (.91)	16.2 (6693.5)	1.94 (6875.5)	2.5 (1.7)	−2.9 (.99)*
−2 Log Likelihood	956.702	823.133	807.638	228.495	377.167	1040.893
Chi-Square	309.495*	460.422*	476.872*	1053.31*	864.119*	176.350*

$*p < .05$, $**p < .10$

Source: Austin et al., *A Survey of Political Attitudes of Blacks and Whites in the Black -Belt of American Southern States*, 2012

neighborhoods plagued by concentrated poverty are less likely to participate in local elections. Poor African Americans are less likely to vote in national elections as well. We also can clearly see a positive and statistically significant correlation between residence in working-class and middle-class neighborhoods and voting in local and national elections. This means that both Black and White residents of these higher income communities are more likely to vote than those residing in impoverished neighborhoods.

Despite their lower rates of voting participation, we also expect the Black-Belt's poorest residents to have higher rates of non-electoral participation than individuals with higher incomes. We find that poor Blacks and Whites are more likely to participate in non-electoral political activities (with the exception of organizational memberships). A statistically significant relationship exists between the "non-electoral activities" variable and the residence of Blacks and Whites in concentrated poverty neighborhoods. As a result, we can generalize, as others have, that poor Americans in rural areas participate more frequently in some of the "cooperative" political activities we referred to earlier in this article than individuals with higher incomes.

Although we have confirmed our first hypothesis, we have failed to confirm the second one. We predict that individuals living in poverty would not have more pessimistic views than others in Black-Belt neighborhoods we surveyed. We discover that Africans Americans from all class backgrounds are more distrustful of their local governments. This is not a surprising finding because national polling organizations have made similar discoveries about African American perceptions of state and local governments. For example, a 2000 survey distributed by NPR, the Kaiser Family Foundation, and Harvard University's Kennedy School of Government found that African Americans were much less likely to trust their state and local governments than Whites were. While only about 25 percent of African Americans say they "trust their state government to do what is right just about always or most of the time," approximately 40 percent of Whites share the same belief (NPR 2000).

Our study also finds that poor Whites, unlike African Americans, have faith in their local and state governments, but are distrustful of the national government. Their perceptions of the federal government are similar to those of the American public across the nation which is dissatisfied with the federal government (Pew Research Center 2010). Because of these findings, we can clearly see that lower- and upper-income African Americans and poor Whites possess views about their governments that are more pessimistic than working-class and middle-class Whites.

Finally, we include the results of our control variables in Table 1. First, older residents are more likely to vote in elections, join organizations, and engage in other forms of non-voting participation. Second, individuals with higher incomes and educational levels as well as married individuals engage in voting and non-voting participatory activities frequently. Third, we find that a person's gender has no significant impact on her or his electoral participation, non-electoral participation, or attitudes about government.

Conclusion

This research offers important lessons about poverty and political participation in the rural South, generally. Contrary to popular beliefs, the poor are politically active as indicated by their high rates of non-electoral participation in the southern Black-Belt. Despite their negative attitudes about politics, they participate in the political process by engaging more frequently in nontraditional methods. Unfortunately, their voting participation lags behind that of working- and middle-class Black-Belt residents. The poor's lower voting participation and negative attitudes about government suggest that they will not have the needs of their community met by electing representatives. Instead, they believe that they must empower their communities by using other means. It is troubling that the socioeconomic group in the Black-Belt that needs to vote at the highest rate—the poor—votes at lower rates than more privileged groups.

Notes

*   We would like to acknowledge Drs. Tracy Johns and Michael Scicchitano of the University of Florida Survey Research Center for assistance with the survey. Also, Morris Bembry, Gloria Bowens, Emmanuel Gamor, Wilneeda Emmanuel, Bryan Konig, and Roseberte Pierre conducted many of our survey interviews. The College of Liberal Arts and Sciences at the University of Florida provided funding through the Humanities Scholarship Enhancement Grant program and the UF Department of Political Science provided a summer research grant for this study.
1.   In 2011, individuals who head families of four and earn less than \$22,350 a year live below the poverty line (U.S. Department of Health & Human Services 2011). In order to determine individual poverty, we asked our respondents their income level, household type, and number of children (or other relatives) residing in their home.
2.   To determine the sample population of the groups for our study, we divide the total population of Blacks and Whites respectively in our targeted communities by our confidence interval of four. To ensure a systematic and representative sample, we first chose an address in each of our targeted communities and began conducting door-to-door interviews. After selecting our first interviewee, we contacted residents in every tenth home to ensure that we had a completely random sample. The systematic sampling technique is superior to the simple random sampling technique because the latter is more vulnerable to sampling error (Carlson and Hyde 2003, 198–200).
3.   First, we combine our "group memberships" questions in Table 3 into one variable that we define as "memberships." Second, we combine our dependent variables measuring other forms of political participation and coded them as 2 for "last 6 months," 1 for "past 12 months," and 0 for "never." We label this variable as "non-voting participation."

References

Alex-Assensoh, Yvette. 1998. *Neighborhoods, Family, and Political Behavior in Urban America*. New York: Garland.

Austin, Sharon D. Wright. 2006. *The Transformation of Plantation Politics: Black Politics, Concentrated Poverty, and Social Capital in the Mississippi Delta*. Albany, NY: State University of New York Press.

Berry, Jeffrey M., Kent E. Portney, and Ken Thomson. 1991. "The Political Behavior of Poor People." In *The Urban Underclass*, ed. Christopher Jencks and Paul E. Peterson, 357–72. Washington, D.C.: Brookings Institution.

Bishaw, Alemayehu. 2005. "Areas with Concentrated Poverty: 1999." *Census 2000 Special Reports*. Washington, D.C.: U.S. Department of Commerce.

Brady, Henry E., Sidney Verba, and Kay Lehman Schlozman. 1995. "Beyond SES: A Resource Model of Political Participation." *American Political Science Review* 89: 271–94.

Cohen, Cathy, and Michael Dawson. 1993. "Neighborhood Poverty and African American Politics." *American Political Science Review* 87: 286–302.

DeLuca, Tom. 1995. *The Two Faces of Political Apathy*. Philadelphia, PA: Temple University Press.

Duncan, Cynthia M. 1999. *Worlds Apart: Why Poverty Persists in Rural America*. New Haven, CT: Yale University Press.

Edwards, George C., Martin P. Wattenberg, and Robert L. Lineberry. 2008. *Government in America: People, Politics, and Policy*. Brief 9th edn . New York: Longman.

Falk, William W., and Bruce H. Rankin. 1992. "The Cost of Being Black in the Black-Belt." *Social Problems* 39: 299–313.

Fowler, James H. 2006. "Altruism and Turnout." *The Journal of Politics* 68: 674–83.

Gaventa, John. 1980. *Power and Powerlessness: Quiescence and Rebellion in an Appalachian Valley*. Urbana, IL: University of Illinois Press.

Lay, J. Celeste. 2009. "Citizenship in Rural America: Political Knowledge and Participation in Five Iowa Communities." Paper presented at the International Society of Political Psychology Meetings, Dublin, Ireland.

Lijphart, Arend. 1997. "Unequal Participation: Democracy's Unresolved Dilemma." *American Political Science Review* 91: 1–14.

Massey, Douglas S., and Nancy A. Denton. 1993. *American Apartheid: Segregation and the Making of the Underclass*. Cambridge, MA: Harvard University Press.

Massey, Douglas S., and Mitchell L. Eggers. 1990. "The Ecology of Inequality: Minorities and the Concentration of Poverty, 1970–1980." *American Journal of Sociology* 95: 1153–88.

McKenzie, Brian D. 2004. "Religious Social Networks, Indirect Mobilization, and African-American Political Participation." *Political Research Quarterly* 57: 621–32.

Morrison, Minion K. C. 1987. *Black Political Mobilization: Leadership, Power and Mass Behavior*. Albany, NY: State University of New York Press.

NPR. 2000. "Americans Distrust Government, but Want It to Do More: NPR/Kaiser/Kennedy School Poll Points to Paradox." *NPR Online*. http://www.npr.org/programs/specials/poll/govt/summary.html

Perry, Huey L. 2003. "The Evolution and Impact of Biracial Coalitions and Black Mayors in Birmingham and New Orleans." In *Racial Politics in American Cities*. 3rd edn. ed. Rufus P. Browning, Dale Rogers Marshall, and David T. Tabb, 227–54. New York: Longman.

Pew Research Center. "Distrust, Discontent, Anger, and Partisan Rancor: The People and their Government." Unpublished document. *Pew Research Center for the People and the Press*. April 18, 2010. http://www.people-press.org/2010/04/18/distrust-discontent-anger-and-partisan-rancor/.

Rankin, Bruce H., and James M. Quane. 2000. "Neighborhood Poverty and the Social Isolation of Inner-City African American Families." *Social Forces* 79: 139–64.

Rosales, Rodolfo. 2000. *The Illusion of Inclusion: The Untold Political Story of San Ant*onio. Austin, TX: University of Texas Press.

Salamon, Lester M. and Stephen Van Evera. 1973. "Fear Revisited: Rejoinder to 'Comment' by Sam Kernell." *American Political Science Review* 67: 1319–26.

Scott, Wilbur J., and Alan C. Acock. 1979. "Socioeconomic Status, Unemployment Experience, and Political Participation: A Disentangling of Main and Interaction Effects." *Political Behavior* 1: 361–81.

Shingles, Richard D. 1981. "Black Consciousness and Political Participation: The Missing Link." *American Political Science Review* 75:76–91.

Swanson, Louis E., Rosalind P. Harris, Jerry R. Skees, and Lionel Williamson. 1994. "African Americans in Southern Rural Regions: The Importance of Legacy." *The Review of Black Political Economy*: 109–24.

Tigges, Leann M., Irene Browne, and Gary P. Green. 1998. "Social Isolation of the Urban Poor: Race, Class and Neighborhood Effects on Social Resources." *The Sociological Quarterly* 39: 53–77.

U.S. Department of Health & Human Services. 2011. "The 2011 HHS Poverty Guidelines." http://aspe.hhs.gov/poverty/11poverty.shtml.

Verba, Sidney, and Norman Nie. 1972. *Participation in America: Political Democracy and Social Equality*. New York: Harper and Row.

Verba, Sidney, Kay L. Schlozman, Henry E. Brady, and Norman Nie. 1993. "Race, Ethnicity and Political Resources: Participation in the United States." *British Journal of Political Science* 23: 453–97.

Wacquant, Loic J., and William Julius Wilson. 1989. "The Cost of Racial and Class Exclusion in the Inner City." *Annals of the American Academy of Political and Social Science* 501: 8–25.

Washington, Booker T. 1965. *Up from Slavery: An Autobiography*. New York: Dodd, Mead and Company.

Wilson, William Julius. 1987. *The Truly Disadvantaged: The Inner City, the Underclass, and Public Policy*. Chicago, IL, University of Chicago Press.

———. 1991. "Another Look at the Truly Disadvantaged." *Political Science Quarterly* 106: 639–56.

Wimberly, Ronald C., and Libby V. Morris. 1997. *The Southern Black-Belt: A National Perspective*. Lexington, KY: TVA Rural Studies.

Wimberly, Ronald C., Libby V. Morris, and Douglas C. Bachtel. 1992. "New Developments in the Black-Belt: Dependency and Life Conditions." In *New Directions in Local and Rural Development*, ed. N. Baharanyi, R. Zabawa, and W. Hill, 77–84. Tuskegee, AL: Tuskegee University.

———. 1993. "The Southern Rural Black-Belt and Policy Initiatives." In *Rural Development and a Changing USDA*, ed. N. Baharanyi, R. Zabawa, and W. Hill, 55–61. Tuskegee AL: Tuskegee University.

Wolfinger Raymond E., and Steven J. Rosenstone. 1980. *Who Votes*? New Haven, CT: Yale University Press.

Appendix 1
Black and White Poverty Rates in Communities Under Review

Location	% Black under poverty Level	%White under poverty Level
Florida		
Alachua County Census Tract 8	46.0	59.7
Alachua County Census Tract 9.02	67.0	59.3
De Soto County Census Tract 9803	36.0	33.0
Louisiana		
Evangeline Parish Census Tract 9506	71.1	31.0
St. Landry Parish Census Tract 9609	57.2	29.9
Lafayette Parish Census Tract 1	46.2	28.8
Mississippi		
Harrison County Census Tract 3	36.9	33.3
Oktibbeha County Census Tract 9504	39.0	34.7
Texas		
Bowie County Census Tract 105	50.9	36.8
Smith County Census Tract 4	32.7	37.3
Nogadoches County Census Tract 9506	49.1	50.0
Nogadoches County Census Tract 9507	55.2	36.9

Source: U.S. Census 2010

Appendix 2
Profile of Those Surveyed

Race		Household Income		Gender	
African American	52.3 (538)	Under $17,000	39.6 (407)	Male	13.2 (136)
White	46.9 (482)	$17,001-$32,500	42.0 (432)	Female	86.8 (892)
Hispanic/Latino	0.8 (8)	$32,501 to $60,000	16.0 (164)		
		Above $60,000	2.4 (25)		

Employment Status		Educational Level		Marital Status	
Employment full-time	84.7 (870)	Some high school	0.6 (6)	Single	81.0 (831)
		High school grad	86.5 (889)	Single live with partner	4.3 (45)
Disabled	7.2 (75)	Technical vocation	6.3 (65)		
Not Employed	8.1 (83)	Some college	2.9 (30)	Married	12.2 (126)
		College degree	3.7 (38)	Widowed	0.3 (3)
				Divorced	1.4 (15)
				Other	0.8 (8)

Household Description		Individual Poverty and Class	
Single Mother	74.0 (761)	Poor African Americans	31.6 (325)
Single Father	3.4 (35)	Poor Whites	27.4 (282)
Mother and Father	14.4 (148)	Working Class African Americans	18.5 (190)
Foster Parent	0.8 (8)	Working Class Whites	4.1 (42)
Grandparent	6.6 (68)	Middle Class African Americans	14.5 (149)
Other	0.8 (8)	Middle Class Whites	3.9 (40)

Neighborhood Poverty		States	
Low (0-12.3%)	31.2 (321)	Florida	29.3 (301)
Moderate (12.4-19.9%)	29.4 (302)	Louisiana	19.5 (201)
High (Above 20%)	39.4 (405)	Mississippi	15.8 (162)
		Texas	35.4 (364)

Total Number of Respondents – 1,028

Source: Austin, et. al., *A Survey of Political Attitudes of Blacks and Whites in the Black Belt of American Southern States*, 2012

Appendix 3
Survey Questions Demographic Information

What is your age?

Record the respondent's gender (male, female).

Are you currently single, living without a partner; single, living with a partner; married; widowed; divorced; or separated?

Which of the following best describes your household? (Single parent, grandparent, foster-parent, or other, mother-father)

How many children do you have under the age of eighteen living in your household?

What was your total household income before taxes last year? (Under $17,000; $17,000–$32,500; $32,501–$60,000;over $60,000)

What is your current employment status? (Full-time, part-time, or unemployed)

What is your income level? (Below $17,000, above $17,000)

What is the highest level of education that you completed? (Eighth grade or less, some high school, high school graduate,technical/vocation, some college, college degree)

What state do you reside in? Louisiana, Texas, Mississippi, Florida

Extent of neighborhood poverty in respondent's neighborhood: low poverty (between 0 to 12.3 percent), moderate (between 12.4 to 19.9 percent), high (above 20 percent)

Group Memberships

I'll read you a list of different kinds of groups. Please tell me if you're a member of any of these organizations: churches or church-related groups, fraternal lodge, fraternity or sorority, service clubs (Kiwanis, Rotary, etc.), veterans' group, school-related groups (PTA, etc.), political organizations, labor unions (No, Yes).

Views About Voting

Now, I'll read you some statements about voting. For each, please tell me whether you completely agree with it, mostly agree with it, mostly disagree with it, or completely disagree with it.

I sometimes feel like I don't know enough about the candidates to vote.

I'm sometimes too busy to vote. It's difficult for me to get out to the polls to vote.

Voting doesn't really change things.

I feel it's my duty as a citizen to always vote.

It's complicated to register to vote where I live.

I feel guilty when I don't get a chance to vote.

Voting Participation

Are you currently registered to vote in your precinct or election district, or have you not been able to register so far? (No, Yes)

Would you say that you always vote, sometimes miss one, rarely vote, or never vote in national elections?

Would you say that you always vote, sometimes miss one, rarely vote, or never vote in local elections? What political party do you belong to? (Democrat, Republican, Other)

Other Forms of Political Participation
There are a lot of different ways that people can get involved in social and political activities. I'll read you a list of some ways of participating. Please mark an X under the correct category if you've ever:
Never
Past 12 months
Past 6 months
Signed a petition
Boycotted a product or place
Taken part in a demonstration
Attended a public meeting or rally
Contacted a politician
Donated money or raised funds for social or political causes

Trust in Government
How much of the time do you think you can trust the government in Washington to do what is right—just about always, most of the time, only some of the time, or never?
How much of the time do you think you can trust the local government to do what is right—just about always, most of the time, only some of the time, or never?

Interest in Politics
How often would you say that you and your friends or neighbors talk about political issues—never, occasionally, fairly often, very often?

Reflections on the Presidential Election of 2012

Voter Identification Laws and Other Election Mechanisms in a Multiracial America

Christopher Stout
Southern Illinois University
Katherine Tate
University of California-Irvine

Following a wave of Republican victories, a number of state legislatures promoted and, in some cases, passed voter identification laws. In 2011, according to data published by the National Conference of State Legislatures (NCSL) (www.ncsl.org), seven states have strict photo identification requirements for voting. In many cases, these laws require potential voters to present state issued photo identification cards to prove their identities. While other states ask for photo identification but permit voting if other requirements are met, the strict photo states only count ballots if the voters provide photo identification at the polling station or to an election official several days after the election. Proponents of these laws argue that voter identification laws will prevent rampant fraud and corruption in American elections. In their book, *Who's Counting: How Fraudsters and Bureaucrats Put Your Vote at Risk*, John Fund and Hans von Spakovsky argue that fraud and bureaucratic failings make it easy for individuals to impersonate voters. They argue that voter identification laws will end these practices and improve the integrity of our democracy. And in 2008, a six-member majority on the Supreme Court upheld strict photo identification laws as constitutional, arguing that states had the right to protect the "integrity and reliability of the electoral process."

Opponents of voter identification laws argue that they are a solution in search of a problem, because voter fraud is not as rampant as some suggest. They point to a number of studies including a 2007 *New York Times* analysis which shows that in the over one hundred million ballots casts between 2002 and 2007 fewer than one hundred individuals were convicted of voter fraud (Lipton and Urbina 2007). Instead, opponents of the law argue that voter identification laws are a subtle way to disenfranchise young, old, and minority voters who disproportionately support the Democratic Party. To bolster their claims, opponents of the laws argue that it is not a coincidence that strict photo identification laws tend to come from conservative southern states and have all been promoted by Republican-controlled legislatures. Moreover, they cite a number of studies including one by the Brennan Center for Justice (Weiser and Kasdan 2012), and another conducted by University of Chicago Political Scientist Cathy Cohen and Washington University of

St. Louis Professor Jon Rogowski. These studies demonstrate that voter identification laws will disenfranchise a substantial portion of the eligible electorate (about 11 percent) and will have particularly negative consequences for young minority voters (Rogowski and Cohen 2012). To defend itself in litigation, Indiana passed a law providing free photo IDs to the poor. But, generally, a photo identification adds a costly burden to the process of voting, and can be seen as a modern-day poll tax (which was outlawed by the Twenty-fourth Amendment in 1964).

This note examines the impact of the 2012 presidential election on the future of voter identification and other election laws in the United States. In this piece, we explore how higher than expected levels of minority turnout in the 2012 election may have laid the groundwork for curbing the spread of voter identification laws. Moreover, we discuss how Black voters' mobilized response to the threat of voter identifications may be used to advocate for more equitable electoral systems. Conversely, we discuss why voter identification laws and other voting mechanisms which disproportionately disenfranchise minority voters may resurface as a persistent problem in American politics.

Voter Identification Laws and Backlash in the 2012 Presidential Election

Many political pundits were skeptical that African American voters would play as large a role in the 2012 presidential election as they did in 2008. In a 2012 *New York Times* article, a month before the November election, Columnist Susan Saulny noted, "times have changed. Enthusiasm is down, unemployment is up" (Saulny 2012). For these and other reasons, African Americans were expected to stay home on Election Day in large numbers. In spite of these expectations, Black voters turned out in 2012 in comparable numbers to those in 2008, and comprised the same percentage of the electorate. In some critical swing states, such as Ohio, Blacks comprised a larger proportion of the electorate in 2012 than they did in 2008 (Gamboa 2012).

Some attribute the higher than expected levels of turnout of African Americans to perceptions that their voting rights were being threatened (Wirzbicki 2012). In Florida, for example, the state passed a law which stopped early voting on Sunday, a reversal of the policy which was in place in 2008. Some argue that the law was passed to minimize Black turnout which was largely spurred by the "Souls to the Polls" initiative in which African American congregants voted after attending church (Mock 2012). Fearing that these additional obstacles were being used to silence the Black vote, a significant portion of the Black electorate headed to the polls before the early voting deadline and some waited in line as long as eight hours to cast their ballots. Despite increased obstacles to voting in 2012, Blacks comprised the same portion of the electorate in Florida as they did in 2008. These results indicate that efforts to diminish the African American turnout may actually energize their voting.

In addition to an enthusiastic response from the African American electorate, a number of organizations were spurred to action by voting procedures and laws which could diminish voter turnout. Organizations such as the National Association for the Advancement of Colored People (NAACP), the American Civil Liberties Union (ACLU), and the National Association of Latino Elected and Appointed Officials (NALEO), all devoted a significant amount of resources to mobilize and educate minority voters about voter identification laws. NAACP President Ben Jealous said the organization was able to increase the number of voters registered by 350 percent in 2012 compared to 2008 (NAACP (2012). The combination of the mobilization effort and increased enthusiasm by African American voters demonstrates that members of this racial group *will* turn out when they feel that their voting rights are being curtailed.

Many attribute Barack Obama's success in 2012 to high levels of minority turnout (Bowler and Segura 2011). This in combination with a diversifying American populace may lead some conservatives to advocate for moderation on a number of issues in hopes of attracting the growing Black, Latino, and Asian American vote. For example, Louisiana's Republican Governor, Bobby Jindal, chastised 2012 Republican Nominee Mitt Romney for suggesting that Obama was only able to succeed because he gave "gifts" to minority voters. Jindal, the new chairman of the Republican Governor's Association, noted "we have got to stop dividing the American voters" (Feldman 2012). New Mexico's Republican Governor, Susana Martinez, also noted that Romney's rhetoric "unfortunately is what sets us back as a party" (Hohmann 2012). These examples may indicate significant changes in the Republican Party's racial rhetoric. It may also indicate that some Republicans will moderate their views on voter identification laws as minorities make up a larger percentage of the population and participate at high rates.

The once seemingly inevitable spread of voter identification laws is now being challenged by an energized, organized, and mobilized Black electorate. Their early success can be found in states like Minnesota which rejected a voter identification amendment to their constitution in 2012. While voter identification legislation was a salient issue in the minority community, in a recent survey, over a third of Americans said that they were not familiar with the laws (University of Delaware 2012). Moreover, a vast majority of Americans overestimate the amount of voter impersonation fraud that occurs in each election. Taken together, a mobilized minority electorate in combination with a number of organizations which oppose voter identification legislation may still be able to change the minds of many Americans. This, in combination with the pressure put on the Republican Party from high levels of Black voter turnout in 2012, may discourage politicians from promoting voting laws which are perceived as being discriminatory. In sum, there is reason to believe that Blacks will mobilize politically and turn out in spite of the growth of new voting curtailments, including voter identification laws.

The Voting Rights Act, Voter Identification Laws, and the Future of Minority Politics

In a recent interview with the *PBS Newshour*, Wendy Weiser of the Brennan Center for Justice argues that 2012 has seen the "most significant rollback of voting rights" in decades. While the 2012 election demonstrated that African American voters are willing to push back against regressive voting requirements, there are a number of reasons to believe that voter identification laws will be not be curtailed as a result of the 2012 election. First, public opinion is highly supportive of these laws. A survey commissioned by the University of Delaware showed that more than three-quarters of Americans supported voter identification legislation and a majority of Americans support voter identification requirements even when respondents are aware that the bill may disenfranchise eligible voters (University of Delaware 2012). This result may be explained by growing racial tensions in the United States (University of Delaware (2012). The survey's principal investigators, David C. Wilson and Paul Brewer, found that those who harbor the most resentment toward African Americans were 20 percent more likely to support voter identification laws (University of Delaware 2012). Should racial tensions in the United States worsen, we may see increased support for legislation which could have adverse effects on Black political participation.

Moreover, laws which were established in the 1960s to prevent the disenfranchisement of minorities are being challenged. In particular, there have been significant legal challenges to the constitutionality of the Voting Rights Act of 1965. Many states are challenging Section 5 of the landmark legislation, which restricts states with a history of discrimination from enacting voting laws without being cleared by the Justice Department, in the courts. Section 5 of the Voting Rights Act was used to prevent the implementation of voter identification laws in Texas and South Carolina in 2012. In an upcoming session of the Supreme Court, the justices will hear the case *Shelby County v. Holder* which will challenge whether the preclearance section of the law is outdated and unconstitutional. Should the Supreme Court decide that Section 5 of the Voting Rights Act is unconstitutional, a useful tool to block the implementation of laws which disproportionately disenfranchise minority voters, such as voter identification laws, will no longer be available. This will make it harder for minority voters to combat legislation which will negatively affect voter turnout in their communities. Thus, there is reason to believe that voter identification laws and similar mechanisms to reduce the voting rights and political role of Blacks and other minority groups in elected government may actually increase in the near future.

Black voters should use this momentum to not only push back against laws which restrict their voting rights, but also to create electoral systems which would create more parity in representation in electoral offices. Some voting rights activists argue that Blacks and minorities may exercise better influence over the political process under alternative election systems. Specifically, limited, cumulative, and preference voting systems may provide Blacks as cohesive, numerical minorities, stronger opportunities to elect candidates of their choice. Limited voting can be used in an at-large election system, but instead of giving voters five votes, for example, to fill five seats, they are limited to one, two, or three. Richard Engstrom writes, "The restriction on the number of votes reduces the large group's ability to submerge the votes of a minority" (Engstrom 2000, 32).

In cumulative voting systems, voters are allocated as many votes as there are seats (say, again, five), but they can allocate all their votes to a single candidate or spread them out. In this system, minorities can truly "bullet vote" by casting all five votes for a single candidate. In bullet voting, instead of casting votes for each candidate in, say five, at-large seats, minority voters would cast only one of their votes. By casting only one of their five votes for the minority candidate, minority voters then deny their votes to White candidates, making it statistically more likely that the minority candidate can accumulate enough votes to win a seat. Bullet voting in at-large election systems, however, was banned in many parts of the South to reduce the political effectiveness of Black voters as minorities.

In cumulative voting systems, politically cohesive minorities can aggregate all of their votes for one candidate, making it more likely they can elect candidates of their choice. Cumulative voting was adopted in 2000 in Amarillo, Texas, as part of a settlement in a voting rights dispute. Under this system, the city's first Black and Latino candidates in more than two decades were elected to a seven-member school board (McClain and Stewart 2010, 62).

Preference voting is also called the single transferable vote (STV) or instant runoff voting (IRV). Cambridge, Massachusetts, used a preference voting system for its city council elections, and many Blacks (as well as Black gays/lesbians) have been elected under this system (Engstrom 2000, 41).

In 2004, San Francisco implemented IRV, and in 2010, Oakland elected its first Asian American and first female mayor—Jean Quan—under this system (Robb 2011).

In this system, voters rank order their voting preferences. The first preferences are tabulated, and if a majority of voters did not rank a single candidate as first, a calculation system to identify the top vote-getter based on first, second, and third choice preferences is used. One calculation system is to take the second choice preferences from the candidate with the least first-choice votes and transfer them to the other candidates to see who emerges with the most first-choice votes. The IRV system eliminates the need for a second run-off election. Not only are run-off elections costly to implement, but in the past have become racially divisive, and minority candidates placed into run-offs against White candidates have lost. Run-off elections also produce significantly lower turn outs as many voters generally don't bother to show up to vote a second time. All in all, in light of the continuing problem of racial gerrymandering for single-member districts (SMDs) and the difficulties of minorities in winning equitable shares of seats in at-large systems, limited, cumulative, and preference electoral systems are seen as better alternatives to SMDs and at-large systems. Minorities may consider advocating for more progressive electoral systems.

Conclusion

New laws have surfaced that threaten the equal role and impact of Black and minority voters in elected government. Civil rights and other political groups will continue to challenge strict voter identification laws as unconstitutional violations of the rights of young voters under the Twenty-sixth Amendment and of minorities under the Fifteenth Amendment. States and localities will be freer to weaken the political effectiveness of African American voters if the preclearance provision of the Voting Rights Act, which was extended to 2032, is banned. The evidence suggests that African American voters mobilized in response to new restrictive voting laws in the 2012 elections. Blacks and minority groups should also consider other election systems as a way to ensure that their votes count equally and that their voices are heard in government.

References

Bowler, Shaun, and Gary Segura. 2011. *The Future Is Ours: Minority Politics, Political Behavior, and the Multiracial Era of American Politics*. Washington, DC: CQ Press.

Engstrom, Richard L. 2000. "Electoral Arrangements and Minority Political Incorporation." In *Minority Politics at the Millennium*, ed. Richard A. Keiser and Katherine Underwood. New York: Garland Publishing.

Feldmann, Linda. "Romney Blames 'Gifts' on Election Loss. Bobby Jindal Says: 'Wrong!'" *The Christian Science Monitor*. November 15, 2012. http://www.csmonitor.com/USA/Politics/The-Vote/2012/1115/Romney-blames-gifts-on-election-loss.-Bobby-Jindal-says-Wrong!-video (accessed November 17, 2012).

Fund, John, and Hans von Spakovsky. 2012. *Who's Counting: How Fraudsters and Bureaucrats Put Your Vote at Risk*. Jackson, TN: Encounter Books.

Gamboa, Suzanne. "Black Voters Look to Leverage Their Loyalty." *Sacramento Bee*. November 23, 2012. http://bigstory.ap.org/Article/black-voters-look-to-leverage-their-loyalty (accessed November 25, 2012).

Hohmann, James. "Susana Martinez Criticizes Mitt Romney's Comments, Maps Way Forward." *Politico*. November 16, 2012. http://www.politico.com/news/stories/1112/83960.html?hp=l2 (accessed November 17, 2012).

Lipton, Eric and Ian Urbina. 2007. "In 5-Year Effort, Scant Evidence of Voter Fraud." *New York Times*. April 12.

McClain, Paula and Joseph Stewart, Jr. 2010. *Can We All Get Along? Racial and Ethnic Minorities in American Politics*. 5th edn. Boulder, CO: Westview Press.

Mock, Brentin. "Florida Early Voters Show Up in Huge Numbers Despite Suppression Effort." *The Nation*. November 16, 2012. http://www.thenation.com/blog/170901/florida-early-voters-show-huge-numbers-despite-suppression-effort# (accessed November 16, 2012).

National Association Advancement of Colored People. "NAACP to Turn Out Historic 1.2 Million Voters by Election Day; Registered a Record 432,000 Voters." November 15, 2012. http://www.naacp.org/press/entry/naacp-to-turn-out-historic-1.2-million-voters-by-election-day-registered-a (accessed November 15, 2012).

Robb, Denise Munro. 2011. "The Effects on Democracy of Instant Runoff Voting." Ph.D diss., University of California, Irvine.

Rogowski, Jon C. and Cathy J. Cohen. 2012. "Turning Back the Clock on Voting Rights: The Impact on New Photo Identification Requirement on Young People of Color." *Black Youth Project*.

Saulny, Susan. 2012. "Less Zeal for Obama in a Vital Groups of Voters." *New York Times* A12, October 9.

University of Delaware: Center for Political Communication. "National Survey Shows Support for Voter ID Laws Strongest Among Those with Negative Attitudes Toward African Americans." July 17, 2012. http://www.udel.edu/cpc/research/idrace2012/CPC-VoterID-Race-7-2012.pdf (accessed November 15, 2012).

Weiser, Wendy and Diana Kasdan. 2012. "Voting Law Changes: Election Update." *Brennan Center for Justice*.

Wirzbicki, Alan. 2012. "Restricting Voting Laws Inspire Minority Backlash: Restrictions Now a Rallying Cry." *The Boston Globe* B2, September 28.

Black Politics, as If Black Women Mattered

Wendy G. Smooth
The Ohio State University

By now we are all well-versed with the significance of the women's vote, defined as the number of women who vote in an election and likewise the salience of the gender gap defined as the difference between men and women's support of candidates, usually prompting one candidate to edge ahead as a frontrunner.[1] These two data points captured the attention of pundits and analysts in 2012. Though both phenomena—the women's vote and the gender gap—took center stage, most analyses of the 2012 election failed to note the significance of Black women in fueling both. Only through more in-depth analysis do we learn that the women's vote and the gender gap alike tell a more complex story when analyzed through the lens of race.

For students of Black politics, this election has much to teach us in terms of understanding the significance of gender in the study of Black politics. As scholars, understanding the extent to which Black women constitute the Black electorate and define the contours of contemporary Black politics must shape the way we approach the field. Such an understanding of gender promotes the emergence of new questions in the field and informs how we conduct our analyses. Studies of Black politics and the Black electorate that fail to address gender as a salient category of analysis are not reflective of the contemporary context.

Any articulation of a Black policy agenda during President Obama's second term requires an appreciation for the role Black women played in his success in 2012 (and in 2008). The critical contribution of Black women voters deserves a domestic policy agenda that recognizes their power as a distinct voting bloc. President Obama's own domestic policy agenda and any demands made of the Administration in the name of Blacks require attentiveness to the specific needs and conditions of Black women. Overall, the 2012 election necessitates the practice and study of Black politics as if Black women really mattered, because it is beyond question that they do.

Persistence of the *Black* Gender Gap

A definitive Black gender gap emerged in the 2012 presidential election in which Black women and men's voting patterns differed. As was the case in 2008, Black women again made history in 2012 with the highest turnout rates of all racial, ethnic, and gender groups, and they were the most supportive of the president. A nine-point gender gap emerged between Black men and women with 96 percent of Black women supporting the president as compared to 87 percent of Black men.[2] This substantial percentage point difference between Black men and women's support of the Democratic candidate is in keeping with previous presidential elections. Likewise, Black women's share of the Black vote in 2012 was considerably higher than Black men's share creating a gap in voter turnout as well. When the 13 percent of the electorate that Blacks comprised is disaggregated by gender, we begin to see the impact of Black women voters, as they comprised 8 percent of the Black vote compared to Black men's 5 percent. More Black women are voting, and Black women support Democratic candidates at higher rates. This is not a new phenomenon in Black politics, but certainly an underappreciated one.

In 2012, the gendered differences in turnout and support for President Obama mattered most in the key battleground states of Florida, Michigan, Ohio, and Virginia, all of which Obama carried. In each of these states, the Black share of the vote increased significantly from 2008 to 2012.[3] In Ohio for example, the Black vote increased from 11 percent in 2008 to 15 percent in 2012. Black women comprised 8 percent of the state's electorate and 97 percent of Black women cast their ballots in favor of President Obama. In Ohio, Black women solidified his triumph in this key battleground state.

Black women's strong support of Democratic candidates is by far one of the most overlooked patterns in presidential politics. In every election since 1996, Black women voters have made a critical difference in presidential politics.[4] Democratic Party candidates' success in carrying the Black vote is due in large measure to Black women's support.

Gendered Get-Out-the-Vote Mobilizations

Realizing that an Obama second term hinged on get-out-the-vote (GOTV) strategies, concerted efforts focused on increasing the turnout of Black men. Organizations like blackmenvote.org focused on increasing turnout among Black men between the ages of eighteen and thirty-four, particularly in the two battleground states—Ohio and Virginia. They designed gender-specific messages using celebrity personalities that resonated most with the demographic, and their GOTV strategy focused on the places young Black men frequent. In ads running on urban radio, celebrity-activist turned political pundit, Jeff Johnson encouraged Black men to "do their part" to re-elect the president while acknowledging, "Sisters are doing their part."

In pushing to increase Black men's turnout, the organization's website used a more alarming tone that mobilized Black men with more retrogressive, paternalistic overtures reminiscent of a million man march-style rhetoric. Using interviews with local DJs, community activists, celebrities, and business owners, the rationale for increasing Black men's voter turnout centered on Black men needing to assume their leadership roles in the Black community. This suggestion that Black men needed to regain their leadership in the community, insinuated that Black women's leadership in voter activism reflects a distorted or misaligned Black politics such that Black men needed to set things right by reclaiming their rightful reigns of leadership.

Certainly, the goal of blackmenvote.org and other GOTV mobilization efforts aimed at Black men are admirable, and increasing Black men's political participation in keeping with Black women's participation only strengthens Black community power. However, gender politics are often tricky. Any effort that undermines or seeks to delegitimize Black women's leadership does not represent a progressive politics, nor does it honor the significant contributions of Black women in ensuring Black voting power.

Black Politics and a Black Political Agenda, as if Black Women Mattered

Black women's contributions to the election of the first Black president and his subsequent re-election cannot be denied. Nor can scholars overlook the persistence of the Black gender gap. Despite the realities of Black women's political participation, they remain understudied. In thinking through the state of Black politics, we must note as well that Black women are enhancing Black political power as elected officials at every rung from congress to state and municipal offices. Black women are making breakthroughs even when the fortunes of the Democratic Party are most sparse. For example, in the critical 2010 congressional midterm elections, women of color provided the rare cause for celebration. All four of the newcomers to the House in 2010 were women of color, and three of the four were African American women, a rare bright spot for Democrats in the midterm. Black women have continued to grow their numbers as elected officials, particularly in state legislatures, where white women's numbers have stagnated.

In order to capture the essence of contemporary Black politics, it is necessary to make connections between Black women's power as voters and the growing numbers of Black women elected officials. We continue to articulate Black policy agendas that are not reflective of Black women's material realities. Black politics practiced as if Black women matter requires new approaches to what constitute Black issues.

Many Black scholars and pundits have called for a full frontal overhaul of the criminal justice system as a central component of Obama's second term and a key pillar of the Black agenda going forward. A Black political agenda, as if Black women mattered, articulates criminal justice system reforms that take into account the astonishing growth in the incarceration rates of Black women and girls. It also reflects the differences between how men and women experience crime and punishment. This also includes some attempt at addressing the plight of Black women who are often left to bear the enormous costs of maintaining family connections while their husbands and significant others are incarcerated. Likewise, a stringent attack on HIV/AIDS is essential for a Black political agenda, but only with a keen eye on the alarming rates of new infections among Black heterosexual women.

Finally, to ensure that Black women's numbers in elected office continue to grow, a Black political agenda as if Black women matter emphasizes early support of Black women candidates; active recruitment of Black women to run in open seats where they have the very best chances for success; and an insistence that the Democratic Party support emerging Black women candidates sooner rather than later in local elections.

The terrain of Black politics is shifting. Black women are no longer the "behind the scenes organizers"; those who organize, yet do not lead. It's high time we develop a Black policy agenda that reflects the gendered realities of the Black electorate and Black elected officials. As scholars of Black politics, we indeed have a role to play in shaping this new reality.

Notes

1. These definitions are taken from the Center for American Women in Politics, Rutgers University. *See* http://www.cawp.rutgers.edu/research/topics/voting_behavior.php (accessed November 7, 2012).
2. Unless otherwise indicated, all data presented are taken from the Edison Research Exit Poll. See also David A. Bositis, "Blacks and the 2012 Elections: A Preliminary Analysis," Joint Center for Political

and Economic Studies, at http://www.jointcenter.org/sites/default/files/upload/research/files/Bositis-Election%202012%20-%20merged.pdf (editors accessed March 22, 2013).

3. In Florida, the percentage of the Black vote remained the same between 2008 and 2012, but the overall number of voters increased and the share of the Black vote rose in keeping with the overall increase in voters.

4. For a full discussion of Black women's voting patterns since 1996 and its continued significance for Democratic presidential candidates, see Wendy Smooth, "Intersectionality in Electoral Politics: A Mess Worth Making," *Politics & Gender* 2 (September 2006): 400–415.

The Re-Election of President Barack Obama: The Resilient Black Vote

Charles E. Jones
University of Cincinnati
Karin L. Stanford
California State University - Northridge

Despite the popular doomsday re-election predictions, the first African American president in the history of the United States was elected to a second term on November 6, 2012. Political pundits pointed to a lackluster economy, high employment rates, and a multitrillion dollar national deficit as major impediments to a successful re-election bid. Moreover, political observers questioned the Obama campaign team's ability to recapture the voter enthusiasm that defined his 2008 coalition. For example, in the case of the African American electorate, President Obama's failure to target specific policies towards the Black community, despite employment rates double that of the nation, as well as significant disparities in foreclosure rates, has led some African American public intellectuals to critique Obama's administration.

Professor Cornel West and commentator Tavis Smiley openly criticized President Obama for failing to address poverty and organized a fifteen-city poverty tour to raise awareness of the issue. Professor Fredrick C. Harris, of Columbia University, argued in his *New York Times* article, the "Price of the Ticket," that Obama's presidency has "marked the decline, rather than the pinnacle, of a political vision centered on challenging racial inequality" (Harris 2012). Although African American voters were expected to mirror the high level of support (95 percent) given to Obama in 2008, uncertainty concerning the extent to which Black voters would turn out existed. Political analysts warned of a carry-over of the 2010 mid-term elections in which the Black electorate failed to vote in significant numbers. Diminished enthusiasm among Black voters was expected to translate into a decrease in Black voter turnout, which would prove detrimental to the electoral fortunes of Barack Obama.

Needless to say, the ominous forecast of Obama's defeat did not materialize. Instead, Obama's historical election, the only second Democratic president to win re-election in the last fifty years, signaled the reconfiguration of the national electorate. In this new political landscape, the White proportion of the electorate decreased from 79 percent in 2004 to 72 percent in 2012 and the Latino vote acquired new-found importance, which underscores the saliency of multiracial coalitions in presidential politics. President Obama successfully mobilized a multiracial coalition of women, youth, minorities, and members of the LBGT community to undergird his re-election.

In contrast to President Obama's lackluster public outreach efforts to African Americans, he explicitly courted other potential voting blocs among his coalition. During an interview with ABC news anchor Robin Roberts in May 2012, President Obama announced his support for same-sex marriage. The next month, the president issued an Executive Order to Homeland Security that would halt the deportation of immigrants younger than thirty, but who were brought to the United States before the age of sixteen. The ideas encompassed in the Executive Order were part of the Dream Act, one piece of the legislation focused on addressing the issue of illegal immigration. The result of President Obama's directive meant that 800,000 young people would not be deported (Tom Cohen 2012). President Obama also courted women voters. On January 20, 2012, he issued a mandate that will require all employers, including religiously affiliated hospitals and universities, to offer health insurance that fully covers contraception. Vehemently opposing this mandate were representatives of Catholic hospitals and universities, who claimed that the president is trampling on their right to religious freedom. Although seeking to compromise with religious institutions by allowing them to provide referrals instead of coverage, it was clear that the president was willing to engage in that battle.

President Obama's outreach efforts paid off. The Pew Research Center reported that President Obama received 71 percent of the Latino vote in contrast to Mitt Romney's 27 percent. The Latino vote constituted 10 percent of the electorate. Women gave President Obama 55 percent of their vote, compared to 45 percent for Mitt Romney (Eagleton Institute at Rutgers 2012). There was an apparent gender gap among White women and White men as well. Forty-two percent of White women voted for Obama, while only 35 percent of White men gave the president their support. It is likely that the outrageous comments regarding rape and abortion made by Republican Representative Todd Akin of Missouri and Republican Senate Candidate Richard Mourdock of Indiana contributed to the disaffection of women voters. However, President Obama seized on those comments, calling them demeaning, while continuing to show steady support for women's issues throughout the campaign season. Furthermore, Obama's approval of same-sex marriage accomplished his goal of generating support from the LGBT population. Exit polls indicate that 76 percent of voters who identified as gay supported Obama, while only 22 percent supported Romney.

Young voters were also an important target group of the Obama campaign. Although some young adults complained of being ignored during the president's first term, they also recognized that Obama's policies on funding for education and health care were very beneficial to them. Popular celebrities canvased universities and other areas populated by young people to generate enthusiasm. John Legend, Alicia Keys, Chris Rock, Anne Hathaway, Sarah Jessica Parker, and Kerry Washington were just a few of those who worked to increase voter turnout of young people for Obama. Those efforts were obviously well received. Sixty percent of Americans aged 18–29 voted for Obama, a decrease from the 66 percent he received in 2008. Notwithstanding this 6 percent decrease among youth voters, Obama soundly defeated Romney who captured only 32 percent of their votes (Pew Research Publications 2012).

Throughout the 2012 campaign, Obama adroitly utilized his 2008 deracialized political strategy to mobilize his victorious coalition. In accordance with the deracialized precepts identified by McCormick and Jones, Obama conducted a "campaign in a stylistic fashion that defuses the polarizing effects of race by avoiding explicit reference to race specific issues while emphasizing those issues that are perceived as racially transcendent, thus mobilizing a broad segment of the electorate for the purpose of capturing or maintaining public office" (McCormick and Jones 1993, 76).

Obama successfully mobilized the non-African American segments of his voting coalition by speaking to their respective policy interests. However, the African American electorate voted in record numbers despite the absence of racially specific appeals. In several electoral settings, indicated below, African American turnout in 2012 exceeded that of 2008.

We assert that a critical aspect of the Obama victory was the resiliency of the Black vote. Black voter turnout exceeded that of 2008 in several key states. For example, the African Americans constituted 15 percent of the Ohio electorate in 2012, up from 11 percent in 2008. Similarly, African Americans comprised 16 percent of the Michigan electorate in 2012, up from 12 percent in 2008. In Missouri, the African American vote increased from 13 to 16 percent. In Florida, African American voters made up 13 percent of the electorate and in Virginia 20 percent. David Bositis of the Joint Center for Political and Economic Studies correctly observes that "African American voters made the difference." He further explains that, "In the past, having only 39 percent of the white vote would have been catastrophic for candidates in the United States" (Stewart 2012). So, what accounts for the significant increase in the Black turnout in the 2012 election?

Explaining African American voter turnout during the 2012 election requires a multifaceted approach, which has symbolic, policy, and cultural dimensions. First, symbolically, Black voters partially derived a sense of racial pride by having a Black person in the White House. This explains why so many Black voters in the so-called Red states, in which Obama had no chance of winning, i.e., Georgia, waited in line four to six hours to cast their votes for a Black president. Second, policy congruence between the Black community and President Obama existed. For example, Mitt Romney's pledge to cut social programs and provide additional tax cuts for Americans in the upper classes ignored the policy interests of African Americans. More acceptable to African American voters was President Obama's expansion of health care coverage and support for education, which includes increased federal aid for students.

Finally, an important, yet overlooked factor of the 2012 Black voter turnout is rooted in Black political culture. In *The Politics of the Black Nation*, political scientist Matthew Holden asserts that, "the wish for defiance runs though Afro-American history, in large events and small . . . and is buttressed by a belief in the black capacity to endure. Also embedded in the idea of defiance is an assertion of an elemental right, especially in a situation where the legal order would deny that right" (Holden 18). Black defiance was expressed and actualized in the 2012 presidential election through significant voter turnout. We argue that the record level of Black turnout in the 2012 election is attributed to defiance in response to a lack of respect shown for President Obama coupled with Republican-supported measures to suppress the Black vote.

President Obama has continually endured racial insults by Republican and Tea Party members. Republican partisans challenged Obama's citizenship throughout his administration. Disregarding any racial sensitivity or attempt at tactfulness, high-ranking Republican Party stalwarts like John Sununu referred to Barack Obama as "lazy" and charged that General Colin Powell's support for Obama was solely due to race. Newt Gingrich labeled Barack Obama the "food stamp president" while Mitt Romney consistently ignored the norms of presidential deference throughout the debates. Republican Party operatives further activated defiance among the Black electorate with their efforts to suppress the vote. Republicans adopted a panoply of measures to suppress the vote, including requiring voter identification, the placement of billboards in Black communities which warned individuals about the penalties of voting fraud, and the termination of the long-held church practice of early voting on the Sunday before the election. Restrictive voter identification laws were perhaps the most widely used. Proponents claim the necessity of such restrictive measures due to the prevalence of voting fraud. These initiatives were aggressively pursued despite a report issued by New York University School of Law's Brennan Center for Justice, which declared that voter fraud is a very rare occurrence.

Contrary to the unstated political objective of Republican voter repression initiatives, African American voters throughout the nation turned out for President Obama. We concur with Monroe Anderson of Roots-Com (Anderson 2012) that these Grand Old Party (GOP) actions "awakened the sleeping Black giant." Indeed, the African American turnout in 2012 exceeded that in 2008 in several states, which compensated for the reduced support for Obama among White voters. In closing, electoral factors only partially explain Black voter resilience in 2012. While we acknowledge Obama's excellent grassroots campaign machinery and the symbolic significance of an African American president, it would be a shortcoming to ignore the importance of Black defiance against subordination, which has been evidenced throughout history in Black political culture.

References

Anderson, Monroe. 2012. "GOP Awakens the Sleeping Black Giant." *The Root.com.* November 9.

Cohen, Tom. 2012. "Obama Administration to Stop Deporting Some Young Illegal Immigrants." *CNN.* June 15.

Harris, Fredrick C. 2012. "The Price of the Ticket." *New York Times.* October 27.

Jones, Charles, and Joseph McCormick. 1993. "The Conceptualization of Deracialization: Thinking Through the Dilemma." In *Dilemmas of Black Politics: Issues of Leadership and Strategy*, ed. Georgia A. Persons, 66–84. New York: Harper Collins.

Eagleton Institute. 2012. "Women's Vote Decisive in 2012." *Presidential Race, Center for American Women in Politics.* Rutgers University. November 7.

Pew Research Center Publications. 2012. "Young Voters Supported Obama Less, But May Have Mattered More." November 26.

Stewart, Denise. 2012. "Strong Black Voter Turnout Translates to Obama Win." *BlackAmericaWeb.com.* November 8.

Works in Progress

Analyzing Policies Intended to Redress Gender Inequality in the Developing World

Shelby F. Lewis
Vice-Chair
J. William Fulbright
Foreign Scholarship Board

Throughout my professional career my primary area of interest has been applied policy research with an emphasis on the intersection of gender, education, and development policies in developing countries. One of my recently completed projects was a collaboration with Busitema University of Science and Technology (BU). We designed a Gender Mainstreaming Program (GMP) to meet Uganda's mandate for all development practitioners to promote gender equality and women's empowerment. Since gender mainstreaming is a process and a strategy for making the concerns and experiences of both men and women an integral dimension of the design, implementation, monitoring, and evaluation of policies and programs so that they benefit equally and inequality is not perpetuated, its effectiveness depends in large measure on institutional capacity and commitment.

A 2010 situational analysis of gender issues at BU documented male domination throughout the University; so, decreasing gender inequalities and institutionalizing gender equality policies and practices at all levels and in all areas of University life are the goals of the GMP. To strengthen the capacity of the University to achieve gender equality, we designed a professional gender directorate charged with implementing, monitoring, and evaluating the four major components of the GMP, including: (1) recruitment and enhancement programs for *female students*; (2) research, recruitment, retention, and professional development programs for *female staff*; (3) university-wide *curriculum engendering*; and (4) university-wide *training and capacity-building* in order to create and sustain an institutional environment where gender equality is highly valued and where both male and female innovations contribute to social transformation and development. Gender research, gender budgeting, and university linkages are cross-cutting features of the multiyear GMP.

We aligned the GMP with global, regional, and nationally endorsed policies, strategic plans, and reports. Those we used included the *UN Economic and Social Council Report* (1977), UNESCO's series on *Women in Higher Education: Issues and Perspectives* (1998), *Millennium Development Goals* (2000), and *Education for All* (2000), which established global goals, requirements and benchmarks for gender equality in education. Regionally, the African Union's *New Partnership for African Development* (2005), *Decade for Education in Africa* (2006–15), and *Education for Sustainable Development* (2006) linked education and development, and set priorities and strategies for achieving gender equality and empowerment in education and development in Africa. Nationally, Article 32 of Uganda's Constitution supports the use of affirmative action to address gender-based disparities, and the government's efforts in this regard as contained in documents such as *Gender Policy* (1997), *Strategy for Girls Education* (2002), *Gender in Education* (2007), *Revised Gender Policy* (2007), *National Action Plan for Women* (2007), and *Education Sector Strategic Plan* (2007) have laid out the theoretical and practical frameworks for implementing and monitoring gender sensitive and responsive systems and strategies for promoting gender equality in education and development. Extant BU policies and strategic plans provided the starting point for gender mainstreaming in the University.

Methodology

I utilize multiple research methodologies based on their potential for highlighting the best data and ideas for supporting the interests and needs of targeted populations. However, while I recognize the necessity of navigating theories, policies, strategies, and consequences of applied policy research within different political environments, I find that theoretical and methodological orthodoxy seldom fully explicates and often obfuscates both the conditionalities as well as the sustainable remedies for underserved populations in their quest for equality. President Ellen Johnson Sirleaf of Liberia ignited my thinking in this area when she challenged mainstream assumptions about the benefits of integrating women into national economies with a simple, powerful statement, namely: "You can be fully integrated into your economy as a slave" (Conference on African Woman in Economic Development, 1975). This interrogation of "women *in* development" helped me move to "women *and* development" and on to "gender mainstreaming" and questions about how, when, and in what ways women engage education and development on their own terms.

Most of my research projects are intersectional policy studies that are submitted as working documents: reports, position papers, concept papers, proposals, action plans, and development programs. The proposal for the Tertiary Education Linkages Project (TELP) for South Africa and reports on historically Black universities and colleges (HBUCs) and the United States Agency for International Development (USAID), "Women in War Torn Societies," "Politicization of Higher Education in Bangladesh, Niger and Sri Lanka," and "International Education as an Imperative" are typical examples of my work. However, some of my published research predates the popularity of intersectional analysis and reflects my struggle to eschew orthodox development theories and policies. Examples of this work include *Education and Nationbuilding*, 1973; "Educational Reform in Zambia," *ZANGO*, 1977; "African Women and National Development," *Comparative Perspectives of Third World Women*, B. Lindsey, ed., 1979; "Towards a Liberationist Ideology, *Growth of the American Polity*," Shanley & Lewis, eds., 1983; and "Achieving Sex Equity for Minority Women," *Handbook for Achieving Sex Equity through Education,* S. Klein, ed., 1985.

Inspiration and Motivation

I engage in applied policy research because of its potential for improving the conditions of African peoples. My interest in this area began when I was a very young scholar working on USAID projects in Uganda in the 1960s, starting with the Teachers for East Africa (TEA) project, which enabled me to teach history and geography at Nabumali High School and work with seasoned British, Ugandan, and American teachers (1962–64). I was subsequently recruited to serve as Director of Guidance at the Tororo Girls' School Project (1965–67). Although I studied African history and politics prior to assuming these positions, I had absolutely no formal teacher training and only one year of experience as a graduate teaching assistant. The learning curve was steep, but the teaching load was light. Colleagues were supportive, and students were eager to learn. I spent a lot of time preparing for classes, listening, observing, and absorbing pedagogical methods, institutional and local culture, and national politics. During these transformative years, I was struck by the impact of intersecting gender, education, and development policies on the students, schools, communities, and nations of East Africa. The lessons learned from these USAID projects continue to inform my research and teaching. Ironically, fifty years later, I am working with TEA alumni on a project to help Tororo Girls' School meet Uganda's mandatory "science for all" policy.

I find applied policy research quite challenging because national policies are constantly changing. And, this change does not always move in a positive direction. It is often shaped by bureaucratic hurdles and roadblocks that frustrate and impede progress. However, frequent successful outcomes encourage me to stay in the game at least to this extent. In the past three decades I have worked with a number of members of the National Conference of Black Political Scientists (NCOBPS) on applied research projects. These colleagues generally find the field interesting and feel well compensated professionally for their efforts. I would encourage young scholars to explore the global marketplace of intersectional policies and practices where they can contribute to the base of academic knowledge and at the same time help more practically to improve the conditions of underserved populations.

Influences

Jewel Limar Prestage has been the strongest influence on my academic career. Since my undergraduate years at Southern University, she has inspired and nurtured my interest in women and politics and supported my focus on gender, education, and development policies and practices. She and Patricia McFadden, Patricia Hill Collins, Bonnie Thornton Dill, among others, inform my research as they continue to expand the boundaries of intersectionality to global policies and theoretical resources that meet the challenges facing Africans and African Americans.

Readership

Policy-makers and international development administrators are the primary readers of applied policy research findings. However, university scholars; women's organizations; Pan-African intellectuals; and gender, education, and development consultants, many of whom are political scientists, are also readers on a secondary plane.

Disciplinary Categories

I believe that applied intersectional policy research can be slotted across multiple disciplines and sub-disciplines, including development studies, global studies, women and gender studies, politics and education, public policy, African politics, comparative politics, and Pan-African studies.

Upcoming Research

I am currently working on a project that examines the relationship between educational and cultural exchange programs and US foreign policy. The research grows out of my service on the J.W. Fulbright Foreign Scholarship Board, which supervises Fulbright Programs in 155 countries. I am particularly concerned about the structural, regional, and procedural inequalities in the Fulbright Program, but given the status of the Fulbright brand, deconstruction and change will not be easy. However, national and global demographics, communications technology, globalization, and new political realities demand that we rethink, reimagine, and retool the Fulbright Program so that it serves the nation well in the twenty-first century.

Uncharted Territory: *Jim Crow* Violence in Comparative Perspective

Melissa Nobles
Massachusetts Institute of Technology

I am a scholar of comparative politics who consciously includes the United States in my study. This is not surprising. I study racial politics, and American experiences often serve as explicit or, more often, implicit referents for assessments about the nature of racial politics in other countries. In my first book, *Shades of Citizenship* (2000), I analyzed how Brazilians compared racial politics in the two countries and judged, until very recently, Brazil more favorably. However, the central focus of that book was the ideological and political origins of racial categories and the production of demographic data over time. In my research, I use qualitative methods, largely based in history. While I recognize the utility and power of statistical data and methods, I am much more interested in the origins of data. In many instances, statistics conceal as much as they purport to illuminate.

My current project on racial violence in the U.S. South again returns to these basic issues and concerns about history and data. This project's origins are in the comparative democratization and transitional justice literatures within comparative politics. The description of the American South during *Jim Crow* years as undemocratic or authoritarian is not widely embraced within the wider public, although such a descriptor is relatively uncontroversial in scholarly writing. Within the comparative democratization literature, there is robust and growing literature on "sub-authoritarianism," which focuses on authoritarian enclaves within nominally democratic states. Conceptualizing the South in this way allows for a richer analysis of the region's politics within a larger comparative perspective. To be sure, sub-authoritarian enclaves differ from authoritarian states in important ways. Yet, on the issue of violence, when enclave authorities and citizens, in effect, make their own rules by defying central authorities, this distinction is largely insignificant. Or, at least that is what I think now. As this project develops, I expect that my views will be revised and sharpened.

Much of the American political science literature about *Jim Crow*, with its emphasis on its basic undemocratic nature, has largely focused on disenfranchisement of Blacks and poor Whites, and the instability of politics, described famously by V.O. Key as "factional" politics within one-party rule. But, as Key described, the central motivations for authoritarian rule rested largely on the "Negro's [subordinate] position." His point pertained to the organization of political authority. But, subordination was ensured by violent repression and coercion, as in all authoritarian regimes. On this point, scholars have paid far less attention. The relative lack of scholarship about coercion and violence stands in sharp contrast to writings about (sub)authoritarianism in Latin America and elsewhere, with which the United States can be compared.

At this project's earliest stages, I imagined that it would be a comparative study of the efficacy of transitional justice measures in recently democratizing countries. A contribution, then, was going to be the inclusion of the American South as one of my cases. The project was going to be forward-looking. However, I came to realize that using the U.S. South would be difficult. These difficulties are both conceptual and empirical. I have already alluded to a key conceptual difficulty: the utility of the "authoritarian enclave" idea. The empirical difficulty is rooted in the determining the scope and nature of violence in the U.S. South. For other countries, data about violence are available. This includes violence committed by state or quasi-state actors and/or by private citizens for political reasons. To be sure, these data are contested. There are ongoing arguments about how many people were killed in Chile under Pinochet or in apartheid South Africa, and who the perpetrators were. When beginning this project, I thought it would be fairly easy to find data about violence. From there, I would compare and contrast U.S. violence to authoritarian violence in other regions. To my shock and deep dismay, no such data set exists.

As we know, violence played a central role in the political repression of Blacks. Accurate information about the numbers of victims, purveyors, and the crimes committed is largely unavailable, as far as I can tell. The practice of lynching is the most studied, if largely because of its ritualized and performative nature. Tolnay and Beck (1995, 17) estimate that between 1880 and 1930, at least 2,462 Black men, women, and children were lynched in the American South. But beyond the grotesque and spectacular, the region was characterized by ordinary violence and restrictions of racial hierarchy and norms. Of this violence, very little is known.

I have decided, as a first cut, to analyze racially motivated murders as they were reported in the *New York Times* and Black major national weeklies that have been recently digitized. I have also consulted the archives of the National Association for the Advancement of Colored People (NAACP) (specifically the "lynching files") for more information about violence, including post-1930 lynchings and other kinds of racial murders, which were scarcely reported, if at all. Finally, I have consulted the Department of Justice files on civil rights. In light of NAACP efforts to pass anti-lynching legislation in the 1930s, ordinary citizens wrote directly to President Roosevelt. These letters were then forwarded to the Department of Justice. The vast majority of these letters were part of organizational letter-writing drives. However, I did find a few letters imploring Roosevelt to investigate the murders of sons and husbands. These murders were not reported in either Black national weeklies or in local papers, as far as I have determined. In fact, I have passed two of my discoveries to Northeastern University's School of Law's Civil Rights and Restorative Justice Program, where law students delve deeper into establishing the facts of such murder(s) and attempt to locate family members.

In consulting with historians and sociologists who collect and analyze homicide data, there are no databases of post-reconstruction racial murders until the 1960s in the South, with the exception of lynchings. Tolnay and Beck's (1995) widely used database is based on the newspaper clipping files compiled by Tuskegee University and the NAACP, which Tolnay and Beck cleaned up by locating supporting evidence. Moreover, several monographs of particular lynchings supplement their database. But, the study of post-reconstruction (non-lynching) racial violence is, as one scholar described it, largely "uncharted territory." In this project, I am attempting to chart this territory, in a limited way. There are significant strengths and shortcomings to my approach. The main strength is that newspapers are more reliable than official government records. Often times, county coroner or police reports did not include either the racial identification of the perpetrator(s) or victim(s). A clerk may have decided to include such information, but this inclusion was irregular and not a matter of policy. Furthermore, use of these newspapers is made possible by their recent digitization, making them easily searchable. The main problems, of course, are that of incomplete data and of bias. A more comprehensive data record requires substantial financial and scholarly investments. As mentioned, an insurmountable problem is the basic lack of information in existing original records (coroner's reports, police reports, etc.). Moreover, there are likely numerous murders that were never accounted for, even in official records or in newspapers. A related problem is that although many southern state newspapers have very recently been digitized, they are not yet online, thereby requiring site visits. This research is possible through coordinated efforts. The second issue is one of bias. The major national (weekly) papers reported these cases because they were widely perceived as racially motivated. But, there were likely many other cases where racial motivations were not as readily apparent or discerned with such certainty. After spending this summer in the archives, I have concluded that, in building this database, I will be contributing more to our knowledge about the nature of racial violence than to our knowledge of its scope. There is simply too much missing information about racial violence to say anything definitive about its scope.

As mentioned, I was motivated to take up this project in order to contribute to the comparative democratization literature within comparative politics. A common question shared by virtually all democratizing states is how much political attention should be paid to the authoritarian past. At its starkest, this question is posed to incoming leaders who must decide whether to "forgive and forget" or "prosecute and punish" authoritarian rulers for state crimes. But, it is also posed in everyday life, as ordinary citizens decide where the repressive past fits in their views of their lives, and political elites decide where it fits in political strategies. Scholars also play a crucial role in this often highly contested process of narrative-making. Establishing the facts and setting the historical record straight is never an easy or straightforward task. That said, here in the United States, we have had, comparatively speaking, much less sustained examination of violent repression. Scholars have been content to state the obvious: that life in the *Jim Crow* South was violent. But we really have woefully little to say beyond that.

References

Key, V. O. 1984 [1949]. *Southern Politics in State and Nation*. Knoxville, TN: University of Tennessee Press.

Mickey, Robert. 2008. "The Beginning of the End for Authoritarian Rule in America: *Smith v. Allwright* and the Abolition of the White Primary in the Deep South, 1944–1948." *Studies in American Political Development* 22, no 2: 143–82.

Nobles, Melissa. 2000. *Shades of Citizenship: Race and the Census in Modern Politics*. Stanford, CA: Stanford University Press.

Tolnay, Stewart E., and E.M. Beck. 1995. *A Festival of Violence: An Analysis of Southern Lynchings, 1882–1930*. Urbana, IL: University of Illinois Press.

Political Science Research on Afro-Latin America

Ollie Johnson
Wayne State University

Young Black political scientists in the United States often face the challenge of finding Black faculty mentors and advisors. When I was an undergraduate at Brown University in the 1980s and a graduate student at the University of California at Berkeley in the 1990s, there were no Black professors in the political science departments. Unfortunately, mine was not an isolated experience. Various departments at my two schools did not have a single Black scholar. At the same time, I can report that some non-Black political science professors and many Black professors in Africana Studies saw potential in me and encouraged me to pursue my research interests.

As an undergraduate, I had the good fortune to meet Professor Anani Dzidzienyo, a scholar who knows a lot about race, ethnicity, and politics in Africa, Latin America, and the United States. Professor Dzidzienyo was born and raised in Ghana, studied in the United States and Europe, and conducted pioneering research on Blacks in Brazil and Latin America in the 1970s. He introduced me to the work of professors such as Michael Mitchell, Pierre-Michel Fontaine, and Carlos Moore who labored in the field of Afro-Latin American politics well before their work began receiving the recognition it deserves. These scholars became role models and anchors when more traditional political scientists questioned the importance, and even the existence, of Black politics in Latin America.

Blacks in the Brazilian Congress

In the 1990s, to my knowledge, I was the first scholar to examine Black elected officials, race, and politics in Brazil's Congress. I concluded boldly that Afro-Brazilians were dramatically underrepresented and encountered major difficulties in getting their colleagues to acknowledge the pervasive racism, racial inequality, and poverty affecting Blacks in the country. I say "boldly" somewhat ironically because for years Black leaders and foreign journalists had noted that the complexion of members of Congress resembled that of a European country not one in which half the population was of African ancestry.

I spent the first seven months of 2012 in Brasília, Brazil, conducting research on Black politics. In many ways, this was a continuation of research I had completed more than a decade earlier on racial representation in the Brazilian legislature. My research methods were fundamentally qualitative. I did bibliographic research at universities and archives in Brasília and around the country. I visited the Congress regularly and interviewed members as well as staffers. I collected documents, reports, and other materials outlining their activities, priorities, and legislation. On the measure of descriptive representation, Blacks were approximately 1 to 3 percent of the Chamber of Deputies (CD) in the 1980s and 1990s. In 2012, they represented almost 10 percent of the CD. In the Senate, Blacks continue to represent less than 5 percent. The increase in Black representation in the CD is an important research finding.

Equally fascinating were the struggles of Black members of Congress to organize themselves and maximize their leverage within the legislature. In the 1980s and 1990s, Benedita da Silva, one of the few Black women in Congress, led the effort to organize a formal congressional Black caucus. Despite repeated attempts, she was unsuccessful. Partisan rivalries, ideological and political conflicts, and differing views on the salience of Blackness made a Black caucus unfeasible. Since 2000, new congressional Black leaders such as Luiz Alberto, learning from past efforts, successfully formed two entities: a congressional caucus for racial equality (open to members of any race) and a Black nucleus, an internal group of Black members from the leftist Workers' Party.

These two groups have been the leading forces making sure that recent socially inclusive legislation, to the degree possible, explicitly addresses race. In 2010, Congress passed the Racial Equality Law. In 2012, Congress passed the Law of Social Quotas. These two laws are unprecedented in Brazilian history and have the potential to be tremendous symbolic and material grounds for major Black advancements in education, employment, and healthcare. In 2012, the Supreme Court ruled that social and racial quotas are constitutional. It remains to be seen how quotas will be implemented at the most prestigious federal universities where Blacks have traditionally had a limited presence as students, professors, researchers, and administrators.

Afro-Brazilians in National Politics

While in Brasília this year, I also expanded my research beyond the Congress. There are two government agencies dedicated to addressing concerns of Afro-Brazilians.

The Secretariat of Policies for the Promotion of Racial Equality (SEPPIR) was created in 2003 by then-President Luiz Inácio Lula da Silva. SEPPIR has the explicit mandate to encourage activities and legislation to promote racial equality in the government and society. SEPPIR sponsors conferences, meetings, and events to educate the national population on the reality of extensive racial inequality within all the major social and economic indicators. After speaking with SEPPIR staffers, I learned that much of their work involves persuading other government ministries and offices to prioritize and incorporate combating racial inequality in their programs. SEPPIR's budget and formal authority remain modest.

The Palmares Cultural Foundation (FCP) is the other national government office explicitly addressing issues of race. Founded in 1988, FCP is housed within the Ministry of Culture and is committed to ensuring that Afro-Brazilian history and culture are recognized as integral parts of the larger scope of Brazilian history and culture. Perhaps more than any other government office, FCP has articulated the interests of Afro-Brazilians at the national level. FCP has likely produced and sponsored more events, publications, and other activities promoting Afro-Brazilian contributions than any other government agency. Yet, my visits and discussions with FCP officials confirm that they believe they are underfunded. Several staffers told me that because FCP is so small, it is difficult to meet the needs of the Black community.

Challenges and Possibilities

I am only beginning to analyze all my data on racial representation, the Black experience in the Brazilian Congress, SEPPIR, and FCP. My earlier work on Black legislative politics was published in a journal focusing on Latin American politics. Using my new information, I expect to prepare another journal article on race, representation, and politics for submission to academic journals focusing on Latin American politics. I also plan to write journal articles on SEPPIR and FCP. My larger goal is to write a book on the evolution of Black politics in Brazil over the last thirty years. This project will require additional research but will incorporate the work I was able to complete in 2012.

The challenges of conducting research on race and politics in Latin America remain formidable. The ideologies of racial democracy, racial harmony, and racial mixture have tended to deemphasize racial identity, racial conflict, and racial oppression. As a result, many political scientists and political actors do not consider race a legitimate research topic. For example, I was accused of being racist by a Brazilian congressional staffer in the 1990s for attempting to compile a list of Black deputies and senators. I explained that this was not racist but a technical research project attempting to better understand who participates and has power in Brazilian politics. I mentioned that this type of research is done in the United States and other countries. It is similar to identifying how many women are in Congress and the religious and social backgrounds of political leaders.

Despite challenges, research on the Black political experience in Latin America is growing rapidly. Under the leadership of Professors David Covin and K.C. Morrison, the National Conference of Black Political Scientists (NCOBPS) Race and Democracy in the Americas project began as an opportunity to share our research findings with each other and with Black Latin American scholars and activists studying in or visiting the United States. It has been a productive and gratifying experience. As African American scholars, we need to continue to promote and develop collaborative research with Black colleagues in Latin America and around the world.

Four Guideposts for Doing Research in Black American Politics

James Jennings
Tufts University

Broadly speaking, I continue to examine social policy and community development in terms of race, class, and politics. Much of my work takes place in the realm of public policy in Black and Latino urban communities. Recently, I have also started to consider the nature and impacts of *spatial* inequality in the areas of local economic development and education reform, and to a lesser extent, public health. This interest coincides with re-emerging attention and scholarship on place-based urban strategies and policies for neighborhood revitalization. Though my focus is typically on Boston, I have looked at other cities, especially Lawrence, Massachusetts, one of the most predominantly Latino and immigrant cities in New England. A few publications reflecting my current research include, "Measuring Neighborhood Distress: Tool for Neighborhood Revitalization"[1]; "The Empowerment Zone in Boston, Massachusetts: Lessons for Neighborhood Revitalization"[2]; and "Community Health Centers: From Cultural Competency to Community Competency."[3]

In the near future I hope to publish two working papers. One, "Foreclosure Crisis, Community Building, and Latino Communities" is a case study of how a small Latina-run grassroots organization in Lawrence, Massachusetts, became involved in fighting this city's foreclosure crisis in order to save its surrounding neighborhood. The other working paper, "Black Churches and Neighborhood Empowerment in Boston, Massachusetts 1960s and 1970s: Lessons for Today" is a synthesis of interviews with elder Black activists in Boston who were involved with local economic development through churches or religious spaces in the 1960s.

I would like to take this opportunity to share four ideas integral to the intellectual approach I use in conducting research. First, I believe that examination of conceptual and political connections between race and class, and social policy, requires understanding of the history of an issue or question; related to this, and as important, is not overlooking the history of struggles germane to a particular issue. In some of my earlier research work on poverty, for example, I insisted that understanding historical aspects of poverty is a key first step in analysis of this challenge. What did the face of poverty in US society look like at the turn of the century, or during the period of the Great Depression, or in other periods? How were race and poverty played out in these earlier periods? Insight into the history of a problem, as well as how people sought to overcome problems or challenges at the local level, is important not only for my research, but also for teaching and community work.

A second guidepost for my research and professional work is incorporation of the voices of community activists and residents. I always try to tap community voices and include them into my research and teaching. This is important because there are various kinds of expertise among people affected by a problem being studied that can be easily overlooked in scholarship. Unfortunately, too many in academe have succumbed to the almost mystical proposition that expertise rests exclusively with those who hold advanced academic credentials. A related myth is that social realities—regardless of inherent multilayered and temporal complexities—can simply be put into boxes for purposes of measurement by people who are appropriately and extensively trained. Recalling Thomas Kuhn's classic work, *The Structure of Scientific Revolutions*, this is to be expected in academe, of course.[4]

A third guidepost reflected in earlier and current research is the connection between theory and praxis for understanding how policy and politics are connected to race and class at the local level. In the vein of the much earlier work of sociologist Kenneth Clark, I describe praxis as involvement with daily issues facing neighborhoods, or engagement with civic and economic issues affecting the lives of people and communities, in order to understand the nature and styles of oppression.[5] Linking theory and praxis can highlight information and findings that could easily be overlooked in traditional scholarship. An example, perhaps: when welfare reform to "end welfare as we know it" was passed with the avid support of both Democrats and Republicans, it gave immediate birth to an industry of "objective" research and investigations regarding the impact of this policy on impoverished families. In examining this new policy many researchers focused on individuals and families as the unit of analysis; to wit, are individuals and families better off as a result of welfare reform? Because many of these researchers had little direct involvement with daily struggles and politics in some urban neighborhoods they actually missed a crucial research question; and, that is, what was or has been the social and institutional impact of welfare reform on urban neighborhoods, as the unit of analysis?[6] In other words, how did welfare reform impact the civic and social infrastructure of neighborhoods where high concentrations of families on public assistance happen to reside? Oversight in the initial waves of research about the impact of welfare reform on neighborhood infrastructure in Black and Latino communities motivated me to publish a book examining the effects of such on three neighborhoods in Massachusetts.[7]

Finally, I should emphasize that the sharing of my research and research-related work is not bounded by the ivory tower. It is aimed at the academic community but also professional and even activist audiences. This gives me license, in a sense, to utilize both qualitative and quantitative methodologies depending on the particular policy or issue being examined. It also facilitates interdisciplinary approaches for analysis of a range of issues. Writing to audiences beyond exclusive academic sectors, furthermore, encourages a writing style that can be supportive of democratic deliberation of the problems, challenges, or policies affecting the quality of life in some of the nation's neighborhoods.

Examples of such writings include a number of evaluation and research reports that I have published over the years. Two years ago I authored *The State of Black Boston: A Select*

Demographic and Community Profile, published collaboratively by the William Monroe Trotter Institute at the University of Massachusetts Boston, the National Association for the Advancement of Colored People (NAACP)—Boston Branch, and the Urban League of Massachusetts. This last research report has been utilized extensively by foundations, public agencies, and many community organizations in Boston to discuss not only the status of the Black community in this city, but responses and actions as well. Another recent research report is titled *The Impact of Immigrant Entrepreneurs and Workers in the Leisure and Hospitality Business: Massachusetts and New England.*[8] This research report, based on analysis of census data, public use microdata samples, and interviews, is being followed by another one focusing on the role that immigrant entrepreneurs are playing in the emerging green economy in the states of Massachusetts, Pennsylvania, and New York. Many times, the publication of these kinds of research reports is linked to follow-up workshops and community forums as a venue for sharing data and policy and political recommendations about issues and challenges facing neighborhoods.

I end by stating that I always hope that the approach to research briefly described here helps towards breaking down or at least challenging racial, social, and economic hierarchies in our society, and concomitantly pushes us towards visions of social justice and economic democracy.

Notes

1. "Measuring Neighborhood Distress: A Tool for Place-based Urban Revitalization Strategies," *Community Development: Journal of the Community Development Society* (available online, January 2012).
2. James Jennings, "The Empowerment Zone in Boston, Massachusetts, 2000–2009: Lessons Learned for Neighborhood Revitalization," *Review of Black Political Economy* 38, no. 1 (2011).
3. James Jennings, "Community Health Centers in US Inner Cities: From Cultural Competency to Community Competency," *Race and Ethnicity in a Changing World* 1, no. 1 (2009).
4. Thomas Kuhn, *The Structure of Scientific Revolutions* (Chicago, IL: University of Chicago Press, 1962).
5. Kenneth B. Clark, *Dark Ghetto: Dilemmas of Social Power* (New York: Harper and Row, 1965).
6. An exception to this critique involved some of the work of the late Ron Walters. He organized and implemented several academic and professional forums in Washington D.C., and panels at meetings of the National Conference of Black Political Scientists, to explore how welfare reform and devolution affected Black neighborhoods.
7. James Jennings, *Welfare Reform and the Revitalization of Inner City Neighborhoods* (East Lansing, MI: Michigan State University Press, 2003); *also see* James Jennings and Jorge Santiago, "Welfare Reform and 'Welfare to Work' as Non-Sequitur: A Case Study of the Experiences of Latina Women in Massachusetts," *Journal of Poverty* 8, no.1 (2004).
8. James Jennings et al., *The Impact of Immigrant Entrepreneurs and Workers in the Leisure and Hospitality Business: Massachusetts and New England* (Malden, MA: Immigrant Learning Center, May 2010).

Book Reviews

Marable, Manning. *Malcolm X: A Life of Reinvention* (New York: Viking, 2011), $18.00, 608 pp. ISBN: 978-0-1431-2032-2 (paper).

There was likely more anticipation for the release of Manning Marable's *Malcolm X: A Life of Reinvention* than any Black autobiography or academic book ever. Because of our almost sole reliance on Alex Haley's account, there are literally lost years of Malcolm X's life that we know very little about. Malcolm X is often cast as an historical counter-point to the more peaceful and less radical rhetorical aims of Martin Luther King and the larger civil rights movement. Indeed for many seeking to contain racial tensions, he was also a cautionary tale of an alternative approach to the struggle for equal rights. What follows is a meditation, because it struck me, while reading, that Malcolm X has become a Black folk legend of mythological proportions. He looms large in contemporary efforts to fashion a racial identity that contends with the legacy of the movement generation of the sixties and contemporary racial topographies.

I would argue that, contemporarily, most people are aware of the aura of Malcolm X, the shadow he cast on the civil rights era, and the glimpse we get through mass media. That most Black people have an illusive grasp of the details of his life does not diminish his impact on contemporary Black political thought and rhetoric. He reverberates in the minds of Black citizens from all echelons of society. He has been the subject of movies, screen prints for T-shirts, samples for hip-hop lyrics, and his image is on display in Black book stores, soul food restaurants, barbershops, and college dorms. Iconography around Malcolm X and his legacy is also firmly positioned as a model for Black manhood.

As a modern example of manhood, young Black men mimic his body language and his fashion sense, but more importantly, his image has been constructed as an ideal model for service and living. This is true for men who espouse his ideological and religious beliefs and for those who have a surface understanding based on truncated narratives provided by mainstream media. In the process of historicizing the lives of women, there is often close attention paid to the complicated and strategic balance of the public and private sphere, but rarely are these calculations attended to for men. While many of these narratives are rightly centered on the major achievements of Malcolm X's public life, these noteworthy and laudable achievements are also assumed to be proxy for a laudable home life. A good man and minister, it follows, must be a good husband and father. One who is able to discern so much about societal problems must be able to clearly discern the needs of those closest to him. The logic of these assumptions is clearly called into question in this reading of Malcolm X's life.

Like his subject, Manning Marable also casts a wide shadow on the African American academic and intellectual community. His prolific writing and publishing record puts him in the company of the most esteemed thinkers of our time. It has also allowed us to come to know his intellectual voice and provides a unique opportunity for readers to glean the voices of author and subject. Here, however, I assert two arguments. First, I would argue that Marable's distaste for Malcolm X's political and religious beliefs can be read and felt as a running subtext of this project. I will say more about that later. Second, I would argue that Marable represents a model for a similar kind of manhood that exists within academic settings. Indeed the model of a Black scholar or intellectual, especially a public scholar or intellectual, takes an almost unanimously male form. Think of the proliferation of reading and citations of Fredrick Douglas, W.E.B. Du Bois, Booker T. Washington, and A. Philip Randolph, but less so for Anna Julia Cooper, Mary Church Terrell, and Ella Baker.

I want to talk about the book by focusing on four major parts: a redemptive and reinvented life, a familial life, a life legacy for scholars, and the disconnected source life. The first three are about the information we learn about Malcolm X and Marable's portrayal of him. The last really focuses on Marable and his presence in the text.

A Redemptive and Re-invented Life

Malcolm X had the ability to change his life, to become a different man than the one he envisioned in his youth. It is something people are rarely allowed to do without catastrophic changes or deep fissures in the course of their lives. Enslavement, through its coercive effects, and imprisonment, through its isolative effects, are two important kinds of experiences for the reshaping of Black life. Whereas the end goal of enslavement is to strip its subjects of culture, pride, and agency, there has been a transformatory impact of imprisonment for many Black men through conversions to Islam. Malcolm X is the most important model for this. Recognizing this potential in no way justifies or exonerates the carceral state and its role in dismantling the lives of communities and individuals. Even prison conversions themselves provide an extremely narrow path for personal and social transformation, especially after release and the continuing collateral sanctions against felons. Prison conversions have become so commonplace that they are the source of jokes and derision from all sides. But Malcolm X represents a possibility for social rebirth and redemption even if it remains an illusory hope for most.

Beyond incarcerated citizens, Malcolm X's place in society provides a larger model for reinvention in the Black community. He demonstrates a path for many secondarily marginalized groups that have been written off by mainstream power structures within the African American community. To be fair, much of this is really a Nation of Islam redemption story. They have long been lauded for their ability to take people off the streets and turn them into respectable citizens. This ability is what has allowed the Nation of Islam so much leeway despite significant ideological, theological, and other differences with the majority of African Americans. The ability to remove pimps and prostitutes from the streets and turn them into respectable citizens is their bailiwick. Their presence in communities literally alters the streets by changing the behavior of the people who inhabit them and by leveraging bystanders' awe and fear of that ability to reinvent lives and what these individuals are transformed into, but the limited and gendered nature of that ability has to be acknowledged.

If we take this analogy of the streets and transformation further, two important questions emerge. One is this question of agency generally and gendered agency specifically.

First, on agency generally, it was obviously circumscribed by White supremacy; I found the underlying implication of being able to reinvent one's life critical to understanding the importance of Malcolm X's image. His conversion and those of others like him opened up a door through which many could walk. Marable demonstrates the careful crafting of a public image centered in a politics of respectability used by his subject. People whose lives and life choices had placed them outside of the bounds of community standards found a model or route for redemption to choose another path. That path, however, was an opportunity to restrict their lives (as reflected in their public behaviors) to the highest puritanical and consequently conservative mores of the day. Once in compliance, then their ability to engage with the community expanded greatly. Second, this kind of agency also has gendered asymmetries. For men there are many more options. They are taken from the streets, transformed, and then returned to those same streets as new men with the option to become respected leaders, businessmen, ministers, protectors and defenders, and a host of other positive things. For women this path is significantly narrower. They are taken from the streets, transformed, but not allowed to return. Their image (modest, covered, with children) represents an important public symbol but they are relegated to the domestic sphere. Indeed, their route to respectability leads them quietly to home and not to greater community voice and leadership. If we are to recognize and admire Malcolm X's reinvention and hold it up as a community model, then we must also recognize its potential limits for women. Indeed, using public success as the sole metric for everyone excludes much of women's work in the same way that focusing on electoral politics excludes important non-electoral political work.

A Familial Life

People who follow him tend to be well versed on the trips that Malcolm X took at the end of his life. He was broadening his view of Islam and its practices; he was making diasporic connections with people of color across the globe, and interacting with and recruiting expatriots he met along the way. Thus, these trips are viewed, rightly so, as seminal moments in his life and indicative of the fact that he was headed toward yet another possible reinvention. Because these trips are so often discussed in the sole context of his public life, rarely do we think about them in the context of his personal and family life. Consequently, when Marable discusses Malcolm X's personal and public life in tandem, the toll it took on his family was made even clearer and using him as a modal family man more problematic. Each one of these trips that was so pivotal to his own ideological and personal developments took place within days, weeks, and in one case hours of the birth of his children. As a result, his wife, who in this light is easy to believe had difficulties in her marriage, was left each time with an ever growing family of small children. It is not news that the families of great men suffer. The fact that the work of these men result in the neglect of their families of origin in the service of their larger, more abstracted racial or other identity families is an age-old story. It does require us to rethink how we view these great men as viable public models, but they also become less ideal as a modern exemplar of how to manage private lives. And we are also led to examine this crucial difference between the lives of great men and women in our community. Whereas Malcolm X had the freedom to have a large family and remain untethered in his ability to engage with the public sphere, you have examples of great women like Ida B. Wells who was sometimes tasked to confront the injustices of lynching with child and baby in tow. I mention this not to set up a competitive and contentious dichotomy between the lives and challenges of Black men and women but to complicate the assumption about character that we transfer from one's public life to private life. Instead, I ask us to think about how we often let good character in the public sphere be a proxy for other spheres, and the way we have to use different considerations for how multiple and different identities complicate the way we enter the public sphere.

A Life Legacy for Scholars

There is lots of new information about Malcolm X's life in this book—ranging from the revelation of possible homosexuality, to his prolonged relationship with the White women involved in the crime for which he served time, to the revelation of specific names of New York Police Department (NYPD) and Federal Bureau of Investigation (FBI) agents engaged in counterintelligence and surveillance, to hints about his potential killer. Many of the details have been controversial and disputed, but none of the information suggests a lack of commitment to his conversion and ultimate renunciation of the Nation of Islam and his embrace of Black nationalism at the end of his life.

The most important in terms of political participation was his commitment to building Black coalitions across ideological and class boundaries. Because of Elijah Muhamad's ban on political participation, we often think of the Nation of Islam's political engagement as episodic and self-interested. That is they become engaged when one of their own becomes engaged with a governmental agency, especially the police. But Marable presents a new context for understanding the political implications of Malcolm X's time in Harlem and his participation in broad-based coalitions. We can now ask questions about what these coalitions were like, what was his role in them, what issues were emphasized? Did they all overlap with the stated beliefs of the Nation of Islam or did he make compromises that forced him to overlook the Nation's rules, in solidarity with his coalition partners. Additionally, if Malcolm X was engaged in local politics in this way, would it be worth examining the political participation of ministers and mosques in other cities? So, rather than writing off the organization as non-political because of their prohibition against voter participation, we can look at their political importance in a new way. The wealth of newspaper content, newly discovered Malcolm X papers, and expanded definitions of what constitute the political suggest the need for a re-examination of the political impact of the Nation of Islam.

The Disconnected Source Life

It is clear in both tone and word choice that Marable sees Malcolm X's transformations as expedient. He sees Malcolm X as part spin-doctor, part brand creator who stretches the truth to fit his ends. I think it is clear that there is a certain amount of admiration for what Malcolm X was able to accomplish, but it also seems that Marable finds, in most of his account, that Malcolm X has changed costumes and not necessarily character. It consistently seemed that Marable thought his subject was engaged in a highly public and elaborate ruse played out on a deeply divided America. He often talks about Malcolm X's life as calculated management of a public image. It is as if his life is one of reinvention but also of great inauthenticity.

There are two aspects of this book that are particularly noteworthy. First, the level of detail he provides. Though some facts can and have been disputed, through this work we are given access to more of Malcolm X's life than we get from the overused Haley account, Spike Lee's biopic, and other media attention. More importantly, he provides a tandem story of his public and personal life in a way that "humanizes" him but also consciously removes Malcolm X from the rarified space reserved for few in our community. Finally, Marable leaves himself open to criticism because of the citation style employed. That is, his research notes are not directly attached to the claims he makes. It is not clear why he does this and what is gained from it. As scholars we are all called upon to not just make claims but to substantiate them with evidence. Ultimately, he had to know that this book would be controversial and under great scrutiny, so his not being more meticulous with his source attribution is troubling.

There will be debates for years to come over the significance of this work for political scientists and historians alike. Marable has provided a wealth of resources that detail Malcolm X's life and provide a counterpoint to the Haley account. Interestingly, Marable deconstructs Haley's account and argues for a rereading of Haley's role as more than documentarian and more likely an interested editor. This will be an important legacy of this book because it clarifies and complicates our understanding of *The Autobiography of Malcolm X*. In light of Marable, that designation of "as told to" Alex Haley takes on a more complex meaning. However, he seems less self-consciously critical of his own interests in the telling of this story. Surely, these books will now be assigned and taught in tandem by many professors, and this will lead to a more thoughtful and critical assessment of Malcolm X. This should relocate him from folk hero to practical political subject.

This was Marable's last book before his death and unfortunately we are unable to ask him the many questions that emerge from this work. Left to our own devices, we will accurately assess some of his goals and intentions and miss others. What is true is that *Malcolm X: A Life of Reinvention* is the last in a long line of scholarly studies by one of our most revered contemporary scholars. Indeed, the loss of Marable's voice within our community will silence an important perspective, but his work and the subsequent projects that will utilize his enormous archives will keep his presence familiar and accessible to us for generations to come.

Melanye T. Price
Rutgers University

Gidlow, Liette, ed. *Obama, Clinton, Palin: Making History in Election 2008* (Urbana, Chicago, and Springfield: University of Illinois Press, 2012), $25.00, 192 pp. ISBN: 978-0-252-07830-9 (paper).

With the 2012 US presidential election upon us, we look back at 2008 and wonder what difference it made in the political landscape. The 2008 election season represented many firsts in American politics: the first potentially winnable woman candidate, the first woman on a Republican presidential ticket, and, of course, ultimately the election of the first African American president. The ten chapters (plus an introduction by the editor and a beautifully summarized conclusion by Elizabeth Israels Perry) in the edited volume provide an historian's eye to the political events of 2008. In so doing, the authors—all historians—demonstrate both how far the United States has come since 1789 and how much it has yet to overcome if we are ever to achieve racial and gender equity in public office.

Editor Liette Gidlow divides her slender volume into three sections. The three chapters included in Part I address the representation of gender and race by the media, by the campaigns and the campaigns of their opponents, and by the candidates themselves. The five chapters that comprise Part II put the 2008 election into historical context, laying 2008 over the civil rights movement, the women's suffrage movement, and past populist movements. In the final two chapters of Part III, the authors ask how the 2008 election might have made permanent changes to the presidential election process in terms of financing as well as for candidates who are not White, heterosexual, and male.

The 2008 election gave Americans the opportunity to debate whether the first non-White-male president of the United States would be a White woman or an African American man. Many American women, mostly White, saw 2008 as their year to win the presidency. Hillary Clinton was smart enough, connected enough, and driven enough to finally break the glass ceiling, many believed. At the same time, with a strong candidate in Barack Obama, others saw 2008 as an opportunity to finally tear down racial barriers. In the chapter, "Hillary Rodham Clinton, the Race Question, and the 'Masculine Mystique,'" Kathryn Kish Sklar chronicles the uphill battle faced by women politicians to prove they are "man enough" to be president, while Tiffany Ruby Patterson, in "Barack Obama and the Politics of Anger," shows the challenge for Black male politicians to distance themselves from the stereotype of the "angry black man." Sklar argues that Clinton successfully showed herself to be tough but, by distancing herself from a feminist inclusive style of leadership, she—like many suffragists before her—failed to see the strength in unity across racial divides. Justifiably, as Patterson outlines, African Americans have reason to be angry, but as Patterson also recounts, showing that anger can be political suicide. Obama effectively navigated the fine line between anger and good politics, according to

Patterson, and as president, he is in a position to lead the nation toward racial reconciliation. Mitch Kachun introduces the readers to one more dimension in the race-gender landscape in his chapter, "Michelle Obama, the Media Circus, and America's Racial Obsession." As both a woman and an African American, as Kachun highlights, Michelle Obama was portrayed by some media outlets as an elegant Black Jackie Kennedy and by others as a domineering taskmaster. To be sure, the media had scrutinized potential first ladies for years—most severely Hillary Clinton in 1992—but unlike her predecessors, Michelle Obama faced both the negative stereotypes faced by all professional women as well as the emasculating archetypes prefiguring strong Black women.

The chapters in Part II approach the election from an institutional rather than individual perspective. Glenda Elizabeth Gilmore, in "The 2008 Election, Black Women's Politics, and the Long Civil Rights Movement," places the 2008 election into the context of the civil rights movement. She emphasizes not just the last stages of the 1950s and 1960s, but rather the movement as developed by Black women over the past century. Gilmore suggests that the slow but steady progression of Black women's politics, from association to citizenship to community, created an environment ready for Obama's victory. Tera W. Hunter builds from the latter period of the Black women's civil rights movement when she contends that Obama and Clinton might have avoided ugly race and gender bashing that had shrouded the presidential candidacy of Shirley Chisholm. In "The Forgotten Legacy of Shirley Chisholm: Race versus Gender in the 2008 Democratic Primaries," Hunter maintains that Chisholm, an African American woman, fought tirelessly to destroy the political establishment that pitted gender against race. Admittedly, neither Obama nor Clinton created the tension, but neither did they actively strive to rise above it. Because of this, according to Hunter, the 2008 election did less to destroy the schism between race and gender than it could have.

Both Susan M. Hartmann in "Hillary Clinton's Candidacy in Historical and Global Context" and Melanie Gustafson in "Defining a Maverick: Putting Palin in the Context of Western Women's Political History" suggest that these candidates missed an opportunity to build on their strengths as political women. Deviating from the campaign strategies of her predecessors, Clinton avoided appealing to a feminist agenda and actively sought to present herself as a strong foreign policy and military leader. While Hartmann does not concede that that was her undoing, in saying that Clinton was bested by a candidate with "an ability to speak to deeply felt desires for a new brand of politics," she suggests that Clinton's fear of being perceived as "feminine" prevented her from showing the public her own passions. Sarah Palin embraced her femininity and proudly referred to herself as a "hockey mom," but the Republican Party did not use that story to its fullest. Instead, the Grand Old Party (GOP) portrayed Palin to the electorate as a maverick, a reformer, an outsider who would help her running mate challenge the status quo, and who, by the way, in case you did not notice, also happens to be a woman. Had the GOP placed Palin in the history of strong western political women and built her story as a woman and a rebel, Gustafson advises, the election might have ended differently.

Palin was brought to the GOP ticket, in part, to appeal to the populist Tea Party voters. Running populist campaigns is a strategy that candidates have been using for years, writes Ronald P. Formisano in "Populist Currents in the 2008 Presidential Campaign," and 2008 was no different. Each contender vied to be the "people's candidate." Through

Palin, McCain sought to reach "Joe Sixpack" and "the real American," while Obama supporters were asked to text their friends. Formisano concludes by reminding the reader that while populism can help win elections, it makes governing more difficult. Meeting the expectations of the citizenry, as Obama has since discovered, is a challenge once the campaign is over and the work of governing begins.

The book concludes with two chapters on the impact 2008 had on future of elections. Paula Baker, in "Obama 2.0: Farewell to the Federal Campaign Finance System and the Secret Ballot?," briefly analyzes the history of campaign spending. The success of the Obama campaign in raising funds from small donors, its rejection of money from the federal taxpayer funded system, and the ease with which even amateurs can glean donors' names from the Internet, suggests to Baker that campaigns will become ever more expensive, and more importantly, that votes will no longer be secret. Given history, Baker worries that neither new direction bodes well for the future of American democracy. The future as described by Catherine E. Rymph in "Political Feminism and the Problem of Sarah Palin" is one in which "feminism" is no longer a radical term. Even conservative, "ordinary" women embrace it, if not the issues promoting women's equality.

The 2008 election was exciting, and as the chapters in this volume highlight, it was the culmination of years of preparation. Women have been elected to the US Congress since Representative Jeannette Rankin won in 1916 and African Americans since Senator Hiram Rhodes took his seat in 1870. Yet it has taken ninety-two years before the first woman and 138 years before the first African American presented a potentially winnable candidacy for the US presidency. The road to higher elected office for women and minorities has been rocky and, as several of the authors discuss, filled with the landmines of racism, sexism, and institutional bias. Political scientists have a solid understanding of the politics of elections, but what the chapters in this volume provide is the historical perspective often missed in the horse race analyses.

Of course, there is more to political campaigns than personalities, and how candidates deal with negative media portrayals is only a small, and some might say insignificant, glimpse of how they would lead. None of the chapters addresses the policy platforms of the candidates nor do they suggest how campaign promises might have been shaped by race and gender. Analyses of the election process is interesting in and of itself to be sure, but to truly understand the history made by Obama, Clinton, and Palin, we need to know what their candidacies represented in terms of changes to policy and leadership and not just demographics. To be fair, that is perhaps too much to ask of a single book.

As to be expected in an edited volume, some of the chapters are stronger than others. In addition, of course, what one reader finds intriguing or insightful another might find less so. Some readers will surely quibble with statements suggesting Palin was a feminist; others might be offended at the notion of Clinton being less of a change agent than Obama or of Obama being less a populist than another presidential candidate, John Edwards. Not everything written in this volume is without debate, but that the authors are able to advance the discussion is testament to the value of their work. Will the nation see another election like 2008 in the near future? History suggests we should.

Edith Barrett
University of Connecticut

Minta, Michael D. *Oversight: Representing the Interests of Blacks and Latinos in Congress* (Princeton, NJ: Princeton University Press, 2011), $24.95, 192 pp. ISBN: 978-0-691-14926-4 (paper)

If he has achieved nothing else, Barak Obama's first term as president has forever changed the discussion of race and representation. Michael Minta's book, *Oversight: Representing the Interests of Blacks and Latinos in Congress*,[1] has nothing to do with Obama. Presumably, it was conceived when President Obama was still a state senator in Illinois. Nonetheless, the book's contributions are timely. The election of a Black president forces us to look beyond roll call votes for our operationalization of substantive representation. True to its title, *Oversight* accelerates this search for new measures of representation by exploring how Black Members of Congress (MC) advance Black interests through their committee work.

Although *Oversight* has important implications for current and future research, it is more properly viewed as a response to literature that emerged in the wake of the *Shaw v. Reno* [509 U.S. 630 (1993)] redistricting case. The court ruled that an oddly shaped majority Black district in North Carolina violated the Fourteenth Amendment rights of White residents. Scholars reacted to the decision with studies of whether majority-minority districts were a reasonable policy tool and whether Black members of Congress provided Black constituents with higher quality representation. These studies measured representation in terms of roll call votes, and found that descriptive representation was not necessary for substantive representation of Black interests. Perhaps not coincidentally these findings were produced primarily by White political scientists. Black political scientists immediately challenged the conclusion that Blackness was not necessary (or was even detrimental) for Black representation. They argued that representation encompasses much more than how people vote, and that examining these more comprehensive conceptions of representation shows the value of having Black people in Congress. Minta continues that argument.

Black MCs are essential for Black representation because they engage in "strategic group uplift." Drawing on the insights of the Black political behavior literature, Minta argues that Black MCs are motivated by a sense of common fate with all Black Americans. This interest in the collective drives Black MCs to work on behalf of all Black people rather than just their own constituents. Group uplift is "strategic" because Minta acknowledges that Black MCs are not immune from the motivations and constraints that influence the decisions of non-Black MCs: re-election, partisanship, institutional advancement, etc. If Black MCs engage in "strategic group uplift," then there should be evidence of racial differences across a variety of costly legislative behaviors ranging from constituent service to floor speeches to bill sponsorship.

Oversight searches for evidence of strategic group uplift in committee hearings. The idea is that committees shape both the crafting and implementation of legislation, so Black MCs intervene at the level of committee hearings to ensure that Black Americans' interests are being protected and/or advanced. This innovation in research design is the core contribution of the book. Minta has collected original data from the transcripts of hearings that address explicitly racial issues and social welfare issues across three Congresses: 103rd, 104th, and 107th. Across these three Congresses the institutional context varies from unified Democratic control, to divided government, and then to unified Republican control, and that variation allows us to see some of the strategic elements of group uplift. Quality Black representation is measured as the number of positive interventions that a given MC makes across all hearings in a given Congress. "Positive" interventions are those that seek to protect/advance Black interests. Minta finds that Black MCs provide higher quality representation (relative to White MCs) on both explicitly racial and social welfare policies when Republicans controlled the 104th Congress; under unified Republican control in the 107th Congress, Black MCs only provided better representation on racial policies; and race did not matter for either policy type under unified Democratic control in the 103rd Congress. Based on these findings, we should conclude that Black people are in fact essential for high quality Black representation. Overall, *Oversight* is a book worth reading. It is a well-researched and reasonable contribution to an important debate in our field.

As I stated in the beginning, *Oversight* is well-situated within a somewhat specific moment in the race and representation literature; however, its broadest value may be to contemporary Black politics. The great potential of Minta's work is that he moves us from a strictly legislative focus to consider how the executive branch impacts the life chances of Black Americans. Obviously, that is a question of central importance when there is a Black president. Unfortunately, the book does not fully live up to that massive potential. Despite the title, there is little new discussion about how policy implementation provides different opportunities or dangers compared to the congressional legislative process. Instead, the specific examples that are drawn from the hearing transcripts focus on legislative debates, particularly Temporary Assistance for Needy Families (TANF), rather than program oversight. The third chapter of the book is nominally about the role that policy implementation fights have played in Black politics, but Minta is content to keep this historical overview at a surface level. There was a great opportunity here for Minta to write a *When the Marching Stopped* for the twenty-first century. I wish he had seized it.

The lack of racial differences during unified Democratic control provides another opportunity that was not fully explored. Minta interprets these findings from the viewpoint that Black MCs were in critical gatekeeping positions, so it was not necessary for them to publicly oppose the legislative initiatives of a Democratic president. This is an extremely important insight. A critical question raised by Obama's election is whether it is more important to have a Black president or a Black chair of the Ways and Means Committee—or if both positions necessarily constrain Black politicians from engaging in Black politics. Minta's findings are a great step forward in answering that type of question. However, the missed opportunity was in the negative interpretation of these results: the internal politics of the Democratic Party constrains the enactment of a Black policy agenda.

The argument in this book is that common fate often trumps the other more mundane motivations that Black MCs have. These null results for the 103rd Congress offer a rebuttal: the "strategic" might carry more weight than the "group uplift." If the rebuttal is correct, then Black elected officials are no different than their White counterparts in terms of what motivates their decisions. We would observe differences in behavior because of differences in constituencies and electoral coalitions. If the world operates under this set of assumptions, then a President Obama is perhaps no different than a President Gore might have been. Obviously, much of that discussion would be beyond the scope of this book, but the discussion would have been richer for acknowledging some of these alternative interpretations of the findings.

Minta's use of "strategic group uplift" raises a crucial question for the future of Black politics research. How much further can linked fate take us? The concept of linked fate has become a de facto "grand theory of Blackness." All of us have grown a bit lazy by thinking about new conceptual frameworks only in these terms. Needless to say, I do not have some alternative concept that can match the simplicity or apparent explanatory power of linked fate. However, I challenge us all to push further or at least take it more seriously in our hypothesis testing. For example, if, as Minta claims, linked fate is the driving force behind Black legislative behavior, then what we are really interested in is how Black MCs' interventions vary across different levels of linked fate. Instead of thinking in terms of a dichotomy and assuming that all Black elected officials are on the same side of the binary, we should think of Black MCs being situated along a continuum. That type of approach necessitates a new (potentially impossible) strand of research, and shifts our focus to more fruitful explorations of intraracial rather than interracial differences.

Ultimately, I hope that all book reviews that appear in this journal ask what the work tells us about Black politics and/or Black political science. Minta's work speaks to what I see as both the promise and flaw of both Black politics and Black political science right now. The promise is that Black people have been able to elect their own to important seats of institutional power and Black political scientists have been responsible for spearheading the study of that change. This book is clearly in that tradition. The flaw is that Black people and Black political science too often assume that it is our collective responsibility to keep Black people in these seats of power. Minta begins with the premise that Black representation is valuable and needs to be defended through scholarship. Black Americans begin with the premise that a Black president is an important and good thing that needs to be defended through our votes. I would humbly suggest that the value of Black representation should be measured in how well it has worked to enact a Black policy agenda. On those grounds, we should all start from a premise of failure.

Matthew B. Platt
Harvard University

Note

1. For the purpose of this review I will focus only on Black representation. As the title suggests, Minta provides discussion of Latino representation. The disparity of emphasis in this book review is the product of the reviewer and not the author of the book.

Grose, Christian. *Congress in Black and White: Race and Representation in Washington and at Home* (New York: Cambridge University Press, 2011), $24.99, 242 pp. ISBN: 978-0-521-17701-6 (paper).

Congress in Black and White: Race and Representation in Washington and at Home is a contemporary multimethod analysis about the effects of race on the nature of congressional representation. Grose addresses a major scholarly debate regarding racial representation in the United States Congress by examining the nexus between descriptive and substantive representation. He argues that African American legislators are the most optimal sources of substantive representation of Black constituency interests. Grose provides new evidence which suggests that substantive representation of Black interests vary according to the type of legislative behavior and activity. In both aggregate and individual level analyses, the author empirically examines whether or not substantive representation is maximized through floor voting on civil rights policy, constituency service, or project delivery. He contends that the most important means of substantive representation for Black constituents occur as a result of distributive public policymaking, as opposed to legislators' roll call voting behavior.

While theoretical expectations of the research are clearly rooted in the extant literature on race and representation, Grose adopts a refreshingly new approach and frame of reference for explaining the overall dynamics of substantive representation. His approach lies in developing a unified theory of representation. Standard explanatory variables, including race of legislator, district's percent Black population, and party, commonly used in studies on racial representation are used to predict substantive representation. In examining these factors, the author makes a significant contribution to the body of research on race and congressional representation by disaggregating the effects of the race of the legislator and percent Black population in districts. Grose notes that few scholars have disentangled the separate effects of these factors due to the racial homogeneity of Black congressional districts prior to the mid-1990s court-ordered redistricting which resulted in an increase in the number of Black congresspersons representing racially diverse or White majority districts, most notably in the South (noting the examples of Sanford Bishop and Cynthia McKinney). The growing diversity of districts represented by Black congressperson lends scholars the chance to avoid daunting methodological difficulties by analyzing the influence of race and the district's Black population separately, especially since these variables are usually highly correlated. Further, in outlining the theory of the study, Grose includes an additional factor, termed "racial trust" (the interactive effect between race of legislator and district Black population) to explain substantive policy outcomes. Racial trust is related to differential turnout levels and mobilization rates of Blacks and Whites. In an effort to link theories and empirical findings of mass political participation to minority representation, the author asserts that substantive representation will vary based upon the differences in Black-White voter mobilization rates of Black and White legislators and the Black population in the district. An underlying assumption of the "racial trust" variable is that Black legislators are rational actors and similarly to White legislators they are re-election seekers. Substantive representation, therefore, is largely driven by legislators' electoral support and coalitions. In fact, Grose maintains that electoral constraints are central in understanding the dynamics of representation through service and "pork" project allocation to districts rather than merely roll call voting. He captures the essence of representation by identifying and examining multiple forms of representation beyond the Washington context.

After establishing the theory and parameters of the study, Grose substantively discusses the nature and effects of racial redistricting in the early to mid-1990s and 2000s. Due to the passage of the Voting Rights Act of 1982 and following the 1990 census, Black majority districts were created. The most significant number of Black majority districts was drawn for the 1992 elections which resulted in a greater number of Blacks elected to Congress, primarily from the South. Challenges to the creation of Black majority districts due to claims of vote dilution of White voters led to reduced Black populations in many districts represented by Black congresspersons. A core issue explored is whether or not racial redistricting, prior to and after 1992, affects aggregate outcomes on civil rights floor voting in the U.S. House. Interestingly, the author rejects both sides, liberal and conservative views, about the effects of racial redistricting. He argues that drawing majority Black districts does not necessarily enhance or harm Black interests when considering the outcomes of floor voting on civil rights. Based on a longitudinal analysis (1969–2004) of the U.S. House using civil rights ideological point estimates, Grose argues that racial redistricting has minimal to no effects upon support for civil rights policy. Rather, party is the key determinant of civil rights voting. Moreover, the author maintains that racial redistricting does not necessarily explain the 1994 Republican takeover in the U.S. Congress. Major Republican victories in 1994 are attributable to the electoral realignment of southern voters to the Republican Party. In evaluating the overall effects of racial redistricting on policymaking in the U.S. House, Grose shows that civil rights ideological positions of the median legislator (pivotal voter) (also, the party median on civil rights was unaffected by racial redistricting) did not vary much from one Congress to the next irrespective of whether predominantly Black districts or Black influence districts were dominant and regardless of party control in the U.S. House of Representatives.

A subsequent analysis about the effects of racial redistricting on ideological voting on civil rights of the median legislator of individual state delegations in southern and border states indicated a slightly different depiction from the aggregate analyses. In the southern states (Alabama, Virginia, North Carolina, and Georgia), although small in magnitude, the median legislator shifted to the left on civil rights. Notably, the median legislators in two states (Alabama and Virginia), in particular, continued to shift to the left during the 104th Congress (post-redistricting-Grand Old Party (GOP) control). Though insights are gleaned about the ideological changes in civil rights preferences over time in varied states, a major limitation is the small sample size and the limited ability to generalize beyond the South.

Using regression analyses, Grose further examines support for civil rights (based upon Leadership Conference on Civil Rights (LCCR) scores) at the individual level. Substantive findings indicate that party is the most significant predictor of civil rights voting. While the race of the legislator matters, the author contends that it has a small effect when controlling for Black population and party of legislator, upon congressional voting on civil rights. The racial trust variable yielded no statistical significance in the ordinary least squares (OLS) regression model. Grose is the first scholar to estimate the effects of racial trust on substantive representation measured as civil rights voting. Perhaps, more precise ways of measuring "racial trust" may produce different outcomes.

Based on seventeen congressional districts in the South, the second half of the study adopts a qualitative approach for understanding the significance of constituency service, district office location, racial demographic breakdown of district staff, and pork barrel politics for obtaining substantive representation. In terms of the first two factors, constituency service and location of district offices, Grose found that race of the legislator is clearly the most significant factor. Black legislators, representing both Black influence and majority Black, were more likely to locate district offices in Black neighborhoods. Additionally, difference of means tests suggest that Black legislators disproportionately hire Black staff above the mean Black population of their districts. Similarly, this pattern emerges for Black majority districts but not Black influence districts. Explanation of concrete examples of how district office locations guarantee substantive representation should be explicated in the study.

In addition to constituency service, district office locations, racial demographic of staff, Grose also identifies pork barreling politics as a form of substantive representation. In particular, he examines pork barrel projects distributed to Black counties and to historically Black colleges and universities (HBCUs) (number and dollar amount of projects). He found that Black legislators compared to White legislators were significantly more likely to obtain "pork" for HBCUs and Black counties. Counterintuitive results indicate that Republican legislators seek to deliver service and "pork" projects to African Americans. Pork barrel politics viewed as substantive representation raises concerns especially since benefits, as defined in the study, appear specific and unique and do not necessarily lead to tangible resources for the broader African American community.

Notwithstanding, the study has important implications for understanding the value and validity of racial redistricting and voting rights. Grose offers policy recommendations for the optimal districting strategies necessary to maximize substantive representation of Black interests. He asserts that the creation of "black decisive" (Black majority or Black influence) districts less than 50 percent Black are the most effective districting plans for promoting substantive representation, in terms of constituency service and project allocation, to Black constituents.

Overall, the book is a compelling account about how substantive representation is affected based upon varied congressional behavior beyond roll call voting. Grose incisively argues that "pork" project delivery, rather than roll call voting on civil rights policy, is an effective way African American congresspersons represent Black constituents. The conceptual framework of the study is an invaluable contribution for future research on racial representation.

Linda M. Trautman
Ohio University-Lancaster

Woodruff, Nan Elizabeth. *American Congo: The African American Freedom Struggle in the Delta* (Chapel Hill, NC: University of North Carolina Press, 2012), $24.95, 288 pp. ISBN: 978-0-8078-7230-7 (paper).

Amid an increasing bevy of spectacular historical and political analyses of race in southern society after the Civil War, Woodruff makes another splendid contribution. While taking the apt metaphor of the Belgian Congo, Woodruff documents the horrific violence that accompanied the post-war transition that ultimately resulted in the share-cropping system of virtual peonage for the newly freed Blacks. This analysis is based on perhaps the best-case example of the interplay between the races as Blacks struggled to find their footing in the post-emancipation South. The setting in the Mississippi Delta is within the "fertile crescent" of the old Confederacy, with its pretensions to an agricultural aristocracy. The population of African descendants constituted an overwhelming majority on the land and was almost its entire labor force after the war and into the early twentieth century. So the major questions at this interval were: how could the plantation owners survive the loss of their free labor force and how could the "new" free men and women sustain themselves selling their labor at a fair price. It is this puzzle that animates Woodruff in the study.

She builds her case by assessing the intersection of race and labor on the east and west banks of the Mississippi River, a delta split between the states of Mississippi and Arkansas. On balance, a compelling and well-documented case is made for how Blacks struggled and failed to get a fair price for their labor, redounding to a relationship with their former enslavers that was close to peonage. While making the case is easy enough on both sides of the river, it seems that Woodruff has better command of the Arkansas material.

That said, her treatment in no way detracts from the well-argued point of the analysis—the ultimate, and alas continuing, failure of Blacks to obtain the hoped-for independence in the Delta. But they tried mightily, demonstrating both a continuity of resistance even as they achieved some magnificent examples of ingenuity, creativity, and early success on projects. There are remarkably successful independent African American enterprises developed from exploitation of resources in the region. Just one such example was in timber processing. Woodruff details several successful timber operators who made a significant living from their hard work and dexterity in the use of the rudimentary technology, often their own creations, in the industry. They organized a multitiered labor force and developed networks to supply the market. Their achievements offered an alluring promise of what freedom could mean for a workforce eager to get a fair price for its labor.

Alas, it was not to last. The promise was perhaps too jarring for the planter class that had its own hopes for sustaining its lifestyle of privilege and racial dominance. But it was not just the planters; there were northern investors too who found the allure of the riches in the region too significant to ignore. While one might have surmised that this mix of players would have lessened the violence to obliterate the independent Black presence in the marketplace and to overwhelm its resistance, such was not the case. The violence was ubiquitous and exhibited some of the most horrific elements of inhumanity that matched anything that King Leopold wreaked upon the Congolese!

Meanwhile, in combination with the wanton violence, the Whites exacted further punishment with the superiority of their technology and the availability of cash (or credit). The new technology, of course, was mechanization. The planters and the northern entrepreneurs used their access to funds to both purchase mechanical equipment and to invest in its development. This gave them the advantage of controlling the marketing and delivery of their products. But there was another aspect of technology beyond just the science of mechanization, and it was the emergence of the conglomerate as a structure for collaboration (but only for Whites). In this game African Americans were simply overmatched.

Soon enough the frontier environment of the inchoate timber industry that yielded the moment for the independent Black entrepreneur gave way to the plantation system. The planters, often organized corporate entities, used control of capital and land, and a malevolent will to render the "freed" Blacks hopelessly dependent in the new sharecropping structure—virtual peonage. Indeed Woodruff's account captures how the shift in "the Yazoo Delta from an underdeveloped timber region to a plantation economy in the early 20th century closed the frontier of opportunity that many black woodsmen and aspiring landowners had achieved by the late 19th century, mirroring the experience of their counterparts in other parts of the colonial world" (21).

The violence hardly diminished against them as Blacks continued to stake claims on economic and community independence. On both sides of the river as fast as organized churches, businesses, and cooperatives, *inter alia*, began to flourish, disruptions ensued. Time and time again horrific violence was deployed by the plantation owners to maintain control over this near-free labor. And while the instances of violence were nothing new, the Woodruff rendering is profoundly arresting, detailing the continuity, scope, and utter depravity of some of the acts. And she traces them clear up to World War II, where with tantalizing brevity she introduces the escalation in resistance of the civil rights movement and the role played in it by the returned Black soldiers.

This is a welcome addition to the literature in southern history and American labor history. Rarely have these two stages in the economy of the post-bellum South been so nicely tied together, thus elaborating upon relatively unknown (certainly not well-documented) spaces that African Americans occupied in the transition to "freedom."

Minion K. C. Morrison
Mississippi State University

Rojas, Fabio. *From Black Power to Black Studies: How a Radical Social Movement Became an Academic Discipline* (Baltimore, MD: The John Hopkins University Press, 2007), $26.00, 304 pp. ISBN: 978-0-8018-9825-9 (paper).

For many, diversity and access are critical issues facing the American academy today. Globalization dictates that if colleges and universities are going to compete and survive, then stakeholders must be committed to broadening opportunities for those in "out" groups who are generally categorized as minorities, underserved and/or underrepresented. Administrators and faculty alike are asking how their institutions can be more inclusive and responsive to "out" groups. In the process, they are initiating programs, projects, and processes to address these concerns. Unfortunately, this recent level of commitment to diversity and access has not always been a priority within the American academy. History tells us that this was not the case in the 1960s when African American students across campuses demanded diversity in the student body, faculty, and curriculum, and yet were met with overt opposition to their inclusion in the American academy. Fabio Rojas' book *From Black Power to Black Studies: How a Radical Social Movement Became an Academic Discipline* chronicles the evolution of Black students' protest on college campuses in the 1960s and the rise, fall, and reemergence of Black studies as a sustained outcome of the Black power social movement.

From Black Power provides its reader with valuable insights into the establishment and institutionalization of Black studies as a credible and legitimate academic field. It is a well-written sociological examination of how "social movements initiate change in organizations and solidify their gains" and how "individuals challenge bureaucracies and force them to change" (7). Rojas' research interests lie in understanding how movement outcomes are achieved and maintained. In his quest to contextualize "how the political *fray* surrounding Black studies . . . impacted the educational *field* of the university," (3) Rojas raises two fundamental questions: (i) how did Black studies accommodate to the university? and (ii) how does the institutionalization of Black studies illustrate a social movement's impact on organizations (207)?

Rojas begins the book with an account of events that took place at San Francisco State College (SFSC) in the fall of 1968. The impetus for these events is linked to the ten demands presented to the president of SFSC by organized African American students who listed as their first demand the immediate creation of a Department of Black Studies. This act set into motion a chain reaction spurring the Third World Strike, a four-month clash among students, administrators, and police, which is noted as a "defining moment in Black Studies" (1). The facts surrounding the "revolution" at SFSC are so myriad that Rojas devotes all of chapter 3 to it. He situates the demands for Black studies at SFSC, and other institutions cited, at the convergence of two social movements—one failing to meet the socioeconomic needs of the Black community and the other offering the Black community options for socioeconomic gains. Black studies was birthed out of the Black students' disillusionment with the civil rights movement and their embrace of the radical ideology of cultural nationalism as espoused by the Black power movement.

This convergence of social movements paved the way for students to challenge the organizational status quo within a very constricted institution—the academy. Rojas contextualizes this convergence by explaining that there were three conditions at play that ushered in Black studies and that each aligned with "factors social scientists cite [as encouraging] social movements" (43). The three conditions along with the corresponding factors were:

1.   Disappointment with the civil rights movement and an unwillingness to wait for White assistance which led to a heightened sense of social discontent and the desire to seek more autonomy for the movement;
2.   The rise of groups such as the Black Panthers which heightened the efficacy of collective action;
3.   The creation of foot soldiers, the newly admitted Black students who were the product of demographic changes that created a pool of individuals who could be recruited for a cause and a movement.

These sociopolitical conditions made possible the turning of a social movement into an academic discipline. In addition to the favorable timing, in the case of SFSC, Rojas points to the success of a unit such as the Experimental College at SFSC that made the prospects of a Department of Black Studies feasible. The Experimental College, established in the early 1960s, allowed students to develop and teach their own courses. Black studies courses were among the offerings in this college and the established set of classes revolving around Black studies could easily be converted into a major. So, when the Third World Strike came to an end and the president of SFSC conceded to some of the demands of the Black students, the courses offered in the Experimental College were incorporated into the curriculum of the newly established Black Studies Department in the fall of 1969. SFSC would be the first institution in the country to have such a department.

Chapters 1 through 5 of the book provide a historical overview of how a social movement (Black power) helped build an institution (Black studies) and how the academy, "the organization/bureaucracy," responded to and was shaped by crisis. In addition to SFSC, Rojas' research is based on findings from several other case studies of Black studies departments/programs, including the University of Chicago, the University of Illinois at Chicago and Harvard, which were all created out of the aftermath of Black student protest during the late 1960s. Rojas shows how the cultural and revolutionary tenets of Black power were absorbed into the platforms of Black student organizations and Black student unions. He documents how Black power organizations, such as the Black Panthers, had a profound impact on the political and direct action of Black college students which informed their thinking on and demands for the incorporation of their history and lived experiences into the formal structure (bureaucracy) of academia. Within these five chapters Rojas provides a qualitative analysis of the process from movement to institution beginning in the 1960s with a discussion of the pre-conflict and conflict stages of Black studies. The chapters go on to describe the stages of the development of Black studies with accounts of the rise and fall of Black studies programs in the 1970s and 1980s to their reemergence in the 1990s. Also taken note of is the influence of Ford Foundation's funding of select Black studies departments in the 1970s through the 1990s.

Chapter 6 provides a quantitative analysis based on original research of Black studies departments and programs and the faculty which examines them in order to, as Rojas suggests, "understand how a new academic discipline was created" (167). Some of the findings from this research support what scholars of Black studies know: that Black studies as a field is interdisciplinary (168), is relatively small (182), and that those who teach in these departments and programs primarily hold Ph.Ds in the fields of the humanities and social sciences (184). Above all, there is a significant correlation between Black student activism and the creation of an African American studies program (177).

In the concluding chapter 7, Rojas introduces the concept of "counter center" which is "a formalized place inside a mainstream organization where alternative viewpoints are established" (210). This counter center, he writes, "is the outcome achieved by a movement that successfully institutionalizes outside the social movement sector and within the targeted bureaucracy" (221). He submits that "the chilling-out" of Black studies, characterized by the disassociation with politicized rhetoric and community control of an academic discipline, was necessary in order for Black studies to be absorbed into mainstream academia. He suggests that Black studies' abandonment of cultural nationalism and community education as major components of its curriculum guaranteed its occupation in the counter center. Rojas views this trade-off as a co-evolution between Black studies and the academy and not a co-optation of Black studies by the academy. What it also suggests is that the academy is still protective of its boundaries and even though it has made space for alternative centers for knowledge creation, it is still the guarantor of academic legitimacy.

From Black Power is an important sociological contribution to the sociopolitical history of the institutionalization of Black studies within the academy. Just as Black studies is interdisciplinary, this book is an essential read for academics and students across the humanities and social sciences. The dynamics of power relations and how power is conceded are critical in the sociopolitical analysis of stakeholders in social movements. Challenging the institutional status quo is always political. However it does not always yield the desired outcomes sought by the challengers. Nevertheless, the path to broadening diversity and creating access in the American academy has been facilitated by social movements—civil rights, Black power, women's rights, gay and lesbian rights, to name a few. These social movements are the foundations of the identity-based academic work conducted across American campuses today. The jewel embedded in *From Black Power* is the reminder that Black student activism paved the way for identity-based academic work and its institutionalization within mainstream academia.

Claudia Nelson
Coppin State University

Roshan, Tony Samara. *Cape Town after Apartheid: Crime and Governance in the Divided City.* (Minneapolis, MN: University of Minnesota Press, 2011), $25.00, 256 pp. ISBN: 978-0-8166-7001-7 (paper).

In this volume, Tony Roshan Samara painstakingly demonstrates how White supremacy has continued to evolve in a city that celebrates almost two decades since the official demise of apartheid, having refashioned itself through South Africa's neoliberal security governance regime. Samara's close examination of urban neoliberalism as a "political project and, more pointedly, an exercise of power" welcomes a conversation to critique the mechanisms that fortify the city's security governance (12). Whereas colonial and apartheid eras established violent forms of security that overtly delineated racial boundaries, in today's neoliberal racial era, where market principles become more entrenched in public discourse, policy and practice, security is "a commodity rather than a public good or right, acquired (or not acquired) according to the same logic with which the market distributes all its products" (17). Security, while purportedly sanctioned to make communities safer, in this case, exacerbates a legacy of racialized state violence.

In the chapter, "Security and Development in Post-Apartheid South Africa," Samara examines why urban development programs in Cape Town rely on repressive forms of policing in waging war against crime. In examining the government's attempt to restore social order, Samara says, "the crucial bond between many forms of neoliberal governance is the repositioning of crime from being a consequence of underdevelopment to representing instead, the primary obstacle to development" (25–26). By the late 1990s, two location-specific processes of security governance had taken place in an effort to "develop" and "renew" the crime-ridden city. One was in the urban core where the more affluent reside. Development in the central business district (CBD) is meant to secure market-driven accumulation and growth such as tourism and foreign investment (48). Another is in the urban peripheries that include the townships of Cape Flats, Mitchells Plain, Khayelitsha, Hanover Park, Athlone, and other communities where the population is continuously challenged by the afterlife of apartheid. In subsequent chapters, urban development in these peripheral zones is shown as further marginalizing inhabitants, containing labor, and controlling the population (50). Crime, while only one of the many obstacles that must be addressed to create secure communities, is a priority in urban governance through development programs.

The articulatory force between these differentiated security processes is the construction of a common enemy of the state: the "criminal" who too often is a poor young Black man. In the next chapter "Children in the Streets," Samara reveals how at a time when official reports show investment for the city's center on the rise and crime on a decline, a misinformation campaign carried out by the media allowed street children to be scapegoats for the continuity of crime control measures (60, 77). The racialized representations of Black youth as dangerous and ungovernable fueled a "moral panic" that allowed for the continuation of zero tolerance policing practices, from the criminalization of poverty to coercive cordons, which result in the re-enclosure of affluent spaces reserved for the better off (72, 82). In the less affluent spaces, the "criminal" takes the shape of the gangster who not only thrives on the underdevelopment where he resides, but who is also "filling gaps created by the state" (99). In the chapter "Gangsterism and the Policing on the Fragile Ground of Transformation," Samara offers a brief history of the Cape Flats War in the mid-1990s, a war primarily led by the vigilante organization People against Gangs and Drugs (PAGAD) which took it upon itself to eradicate gangs in the townships. The South African Police Service (SAPS) responded and carried out four counterterrorism operations against PAGAD vigilantes (116–21). At the same time that the war began to wind down and the last operation had taken its course, the Cape Flats Renewal Strategy was passed in 2001 as a direct attempt by the state to eradicate gangs and crime in the townships. Samara presents this to offer a critique of the management and distribution of resources used to reform police and enforce laws, which in his view leads to the expansion of the criminal justice system rather than to adequate approaches to prevent social crime (108).

Samara proposes that better partnerships need to be established among the police and townships. This is undoubtedly one of the most challenging tasks, given that the trust between the two has been damaged in the aftermath of apartheid. It is in the chapter "The Weight of Policing of the Cape Flats" that we get a close account of the normalized police presence and harassment in the everyday lives of Black youth. While official police reports claim that crime is on the decline, Samara's proximity to the community during his research allowed him to observe how unsafe communities feel in the presence of both the gangs and the police. The community is expected to be the "eyes and ears" of police but have not been offered an opportunity to participate in and determine the decision-making process of policing and security (135). Meanwhile, other critical issues such as rape, sexual harassment, and domestic violence are silenced, yet deeply impact the communities (140). As Samara aptly demonstrates, it is the policing of invisible racial boundaries through urban space that fuels insecurity.

If the low-intensity conflict was not evident with paramilitary operations, blockades, searches, and zero tolerance policies, in "The Production of Criminality on the Urban Periphery," Samara makes it more intelligible in describing events such as the water war in Tafelsi, massive evictions and dislocations in Mandela Park, as well as housing problems in the Cape Flats, and the high unemployment and incarceration rates. Not only are gangsters criminalized, but so are those who protest impoverished conditions (165). These are the conditions of underdevelopment that lead to the production of organized political formations, including gangs, as a way to resist and survive. Samara proposes that one way to remedy the formation of gangs is for the state to invest in youth development programs since gang leaders and drug lords supply many of these crucial social supports (169). Also, the state needs to invest in social crime prevention approaches: "Instead of social crime prevention acting as a bridge between law enforcement and urban development agendas, enhancing both in the process, its absence signals the ascendance of a new governance regime better suited to an old, divided city" (139). In Samara's view, urban governance is shaped primarily by a discourse of development that prioritizes the reduction of crime through the elimination of criminals rather than a prevention of the leading causes of crime: unemployment, poverty, and other forms of inequality.

To the growing scholarship on neoliberal racial state formations, Samara contributes a critical case study that works to unmask racial dominance in contemporary Cape Town. The value of Samara's work is in allowing us to understand how a liberal democracy such as South Africa has constructed a neoliberal governance regime out of a need for security and development. The book illustrates how threats to the social order are racialized across urban space to target specific populations and how those processes manifest differently in given spaces to maintain a divided city. As Mike Davis demonstrated for cities such as Los Angeles, São Paulo, and Rio de Janeiro—South Africa is yet another "fortress city."[1] With careful attention to how neoliberal forms of security are localized, Samara also shows how South Africa draws on international models for guidance on governance (131–37). Moreover, Samara reminds his readers that the war on crime is a war against youth, who in the midst of punitive state repression have historically proven to be among the first to rebel. This war has *evolved* over time from the counterinsurgency against rebels during apartheid to the counterterrorism against vigilantes of the late 1990s to the countergangsterism of today (124).

Samara's work primarily falls short because of his desire to find ways to alleviate tension between the community and the police. While he views the lack of police-community partnerships as a missed opportunity, such autonomous community space may not be a great moment of transformation for new forms of governance to emerge. After all the police apparatus will always function as an arm of the neoliberal racial state and the state will protect capital's desire to create a world class city. South Africa's vast territory, its diverse cultures, and history suggest there are variations across the townships in how they envision community safety, security, and accountability. It is toward the end of his book that resiliency is most evident in the same areas where urban development occurs. For example, in an effort to address the abandonment of youth in Tafelsig, the People's Power Secondary School was installed as a grassroots effort for the community to establish a clinic, garden, and classes. Yet, it was unlawfully raided by the police in efforts to shut it down (168). Such realities suggest perhaps that the greatest threat to the interests of the neoliberal state are communities exercising self-determination, producing social relations that do not rely on the state and providing alternative possibilities for communities to determine their own destiny through direct action and parallel institutions.

As scholars have noted, a focus on social crime prevention as remedy still allows for the gangster to be blamed for the conditions that lead to their criminal activities.[2] Rather than view gangs as the problem, we must examine the conditions that allow for the abuse of power to exist. The blame must be shifted from the youth who are victims to those who exercise and preserve repressive state powers that resemble reformulations of apartheid South Africa.

Lucha Arévalo
University of California, Riverside

Notes

1. Davis, Mike, *City of Quartz: Excavating the Future in Los Angeles* (London: Verso, 1990).
2. Randall Collins, "Patrimonial Alliances and Failures of State Penetration. A Historical Dynamic of Crime, Corruption, Gangs, and Mafias," *The ANNALS of the American Academy of Political and Social Science* 636, no. 1 (July 2011): 16–31; David Garland, *The Culture of Control: Crime and Social Order in Contemporary Society* (University of Chicago Press, 2011).

Ndima, Dial. *The Law of Commoners and Kings: Narratives of a Rural Transkei Magistrate* (UNISA: University of South Africa Press and Boston: Brill, 2004), $31.00, 129 pp. ISBN: 1-86888-286-1 (paper).

The Law of Commoners and Kings: Narratives of a Rural Transkei Magistrate by Dial Ndima, a Black African, provides a methodical perspective on the legal system in the Transkei region of South Africa during its period of putative independence (1976–94). Ndima served several rural communities in his native Transkei region. He provides a chronicle of his life experiences in the republic, focusing on 1980–94. The author's overall goal is to determine the basis on which African people can make a specific claim to the validity and appropriateness of their own culture, under the domination of Roman-Dutch law. Ndima shows how Roman-Dutch law has shaped and, in some instances, threatened the integrity of traditional law, and the right of people to maintain cultural autonomy.

Ndima's utilization of the narrative as a mode of analysis brings out the validity of the cultural traditions that, he argues, have been lost by the Westernization of African societies. Ndima's decision to base his analysis on the use of narratives is not without controversy. The use of narratives as a legitimate means for recording history was debatable in Western scholarship. In the 1960s, the study of narratives was advanced by French structuralists probing its use in literary theory and anthropology. In the social sciences, the narrative has come to challenge the purported universal theories of knowledge and history. It provides a guide to understanding the uniqueness of societies and cultures while also preserving what Vladimir Propp (1958) describes as the universal themes of nature and human experiences (Patterson and Monroe, 318).[1] For those from developing nations, the narrative is the method by which knowledge and history were transferred across generations. For scholars, in particular, the narrative plays a major role in cognition as it helps shape and organize the world around us. In this sense, Ndima uses the narrative to vividly recount the conflicts that defined his career and the communities around him.

The foreword and preface of the book offer insights into the author's cultural and educational background. They clarify the conflicts felt by the author, as well as by a majority taught in the traditional African ways. Black scholars refer to this conflict as the *double consciousness*, the phrase coined by W.E.B. Du Bois. It posits that Blacks are expected to balance their lives in two cultural worlds to succeed in a post-colonial society. Africans faced a Western system that trivialized all that was African, including the laws and customs that coincidentally had allowed the region to thrive and advocate for separate development during the late twentieth century. Additionally, the foreword, written by Professor Shadrack B.O. Gutto, Chair of the African Renaissance Studies and Director of the Centre for African Renaissance Studies, at the University of South Africa, provides insight into the importance of Ndima's contribution to the historical and legitimate work of the lower courts. It was the work at the local level that directly affected the lives of rural and urban Blacks and which has been minimized in the scholarly work on the legal institutions of South Africa during apartheid.

Ndima opens *The Laws of Commoners and Kings* with a story about his youth, which underscores his prompt realization that social position directly affects the truth process. Ndima points out that he acquired an enduring commitment to remain cognizant of the social status of the accused brought before him (2). This awareness follows the author throughout his career and plays a significant part in the legal decisions he shares with the reader. However, his is not simply a recollection of illustrious accomplishments. Instead, Ndima acknowledges his shortfalls as when he recognizes the moments he allowed his perceptions to influence the outcomes of his cases. Ndima studied law during the height of apartheid. African customs for dispute resolution were frequently ignored or adapted in ways that went against the grain of a communal society and which favored the individual, thus creating tension between cultural rights of Black Africans and the norms of Western law, with its assumptions about the primacy of the rights of the individual.

Equally important, the author draws connections between traditional family life, community organizations, and the maintenance of Western morality, in reference to the HIV/AIDS virus and other preventable illnesses. Ndima also addresses the use of laws to simultaneously liberate and oppress the people. He argues that both goals were manipulated to achieve desired results by the injured parties involved in the disputes. An example of this point were the cases of deposed leaders and kings who often attempted to use the dualism of the systems to gain advantage in cases of spousal support, inheritance, etc. This maneuvering was also seen in the cases of abuse of Blacks by Whites. Frequently, if an offense was extreme, the White families feared deportation from the Tanskei state and a legal loss of citizenship. This was not a customary law, but one implemented after the Bantu system was installed.

Similarly, Ndima exposes the veiled aspects of laws and their enforcement in South African society when race is a factor. In this regard, he points to the use of corporal punishment for Black and White girls in the school system. Nevertheless, Ndima was not immune to the dualism of the legal system. Like many in the magistracy, the author constructed a fusion between the authorities of Western and customary laws to achieve the desired outcomes. For the author, this meant relying on a doctrine of community betterment, as illustrated when individual requests consistently fell below the priorities of communal living intended for the traditional African people in Transkei. "[T]he tendency to individualize life often results in the distortion of custom" he writes, justifying his heavy incorporation of Western law into traditional disputes for cases that ranged from child custody to murder and witchcraft (p. 28).

The Laws of Commoners and Kings is a noteworthy contribution to the scholarly work related to the legal systems of urban and rural South Africa during apartheid by considering the role of the dual system in the development of a nation and the protection of the rights of its people. The work is also a valuable contribution to the field of political science in that it provides a glimpse into the power systems that existed at the local levels and of the ways in which they reflected the needs of the people they aimed to control and convert to the Western doctrines of community. For this reason, the right to culture in Africa is a prevalent theme in Ndima's work and the basis of remaining, extensive conflicts in developing African nations today.[2] The contested right to culture has been consistently addressed in post-colonial Africa as globalization and industrialization have changed the composition of the communities and family households throughout South Africa.

There are both fiction and nonfiction works written on the legal systems in Africa. They are usually presented from the Western perspective of the White magistrates who elevated their own roles in the community. These stories often fall within two areas: those who belittled the contributions of African laws and customs in favor of more libertarian evaluations and dehumanized its participants in an effort to justify an inequitable system, or the second type, in which the White magistrates are portrayed as redeemers of the Africans who face daily injustices among their tormentors. Through Ndima's work, the reader is motivated to comprehend the struggle faced by those who value the laws and regulations of their ancestors while being called on to interpret and enforce the laws of their oppressor.

The work is not an objective account of life in Transkei. Rather, Ndima's work is filled with definitive terms about both the native Africans and their White counterparts. Through rich examples, the reader is able to identify with how local magistrates were regarded in the community. The narratives revisit the legal disputes argued in the courtroom without any dramatic imagery. Ndima's accounts are direct, recounting the merit of the cases and how the decisions shaped community relations. The author's use of narrative conveys Ndima's observations and affection for his people. When referring to Blacks, the author regularly uses terms such as "organic," "natural," and "unified" to address their time-honored lifestyle under the customary laws. On the other hand, he reserves adjectives such as "disharmonious," "restrictive," and "oppressive" to describe the Western-influenced Bantu and Roman-Dutch legal systems. Ndima leaves little doubt as to where his loyalties belong, despite his chosen career path.

The memoir of his tenure coincides with the time of internal political and racial upheaval, when the Roman-Dutch system of laws and government were viewed negatively, and its administrators with contempt, as the Blacks claimed their right to independence. This collection of narratives also parallels the advancement of international human rights law that included the right to culture and self-determination (see the United Nations *International Covenant on Economic, Social and Cultural Rights, 1966*), implemented in 1976. This context increases the significance of Ndima's work as a primary source for those researching South African legal systems and social policy. Ndima's collection is a worthy contribution to the increasing narratives representing South African life.

Andrea M. Slater
University of California, Irvine

Notes

1. *Annual Review of Political Science* 1 (1988) 1: 315–31. Downloaded from http://www.annualreviews. org by University of California-Los-Angeles Digital Coll Services, March 13, 2012.
2. Culture is defined academically as a range of activities and ideas of a group of people with shared traditions that are transmitted and reinforced by members of a group (United Nations. *International Covenant on Economic, Social and Cultural Rights, 1966*).

Kathleen Arnold Responds to Michael Tran's Book Review in *National Political Science Review* 13: 140–42

    I appreciate Michael Tran's careful and in-depth review of my book (Arnold, Kathleen R., 2008. *America's New Working Class: Race, Gender, and Ethnicity in a Biopolitical Age.* University Park: The Pennsylvania State University Press, $25.00, 256 pp. ISBN: 0-2710-3276-6/9-7802-7103-277-1) but I would like to record a few concerns, which I will keep brief. First, while Tran has assimilated the first two conceptual elements of my argument—asceticism (which he likens to ideology but which I would have viewed in terms of Foucault's notion of discourse) and prerogative power—he has misunderstood my arguments about exploitation and capitalism as well as possibilities for change in the future. He argues that I do not see exploitation as inherent to capitalism but rather more closely linked to asceticism and prerogative power. This is a mistake. I devote an entire chapter to exploitation and attempt two things: one is to explore the notion of exploitation in a neoliberal economy—not to reject this term but to more fully elucidate it, and two, to link what is often viewed as "purely" economic (and therefore private or non-political) directly to the power dynamics of asceticism and prerogative power. This is not to reject the notion that capitalism is inherently exploitative but to more fully expand this notion, connecting it to a specific type of political oppression. I make these connections because of the persistence of the argument in the literature on globalization that the state is receding. My response was to argue that it is not receding, but rather that sovereignty has been strengthened to create a situation of hyper- or super-exploitation. I wanted therefore to tie the traditional Marxist terms to the Foucaultian notions of discipline and bio-power. Hence, my aim was the opposite of what Tran has argued. My final chapter is an exploration of these dynamics under the concept of "authentic love"—a concept that Tran doesn't even mention. Rather, he picks out some arguments—like an allegedly unqualified endorsement of unions or hope for liberalism—to argue that my argument is binary and reductive. But I would say that this review has achieved the same thing in narrowing my terms in the first part of the book and ignoring important concepts in the second half. I appreciate Tran's efforts in his well-written review and he has the right to his interpretation—but I think he dropped the ball midway through.

Kathleen Arnold
DePaul University

Ron Walters: In Memoriam

In Memoriam, Dr. Ronald W. Walters 1938–2010

The Editors

Ron Walters died in September of 2010. He left a remarkable legacy as a scholar-activist. Ron was a stalwart member and supporter of the National Conference of Black Political Scientists (NCOBPS). He collaborated with other NCOBPS members both academically and politically, and he was an inspiring mentor to many.

In 2011, Howard University, where Ron was a professor for twenty-five years, established the Dr. Ronald W. Walters Center. The Center will serve as a focal point for leadership development and public policy research and analysis on African American contributions to U.S. policy, foreign and domestic. It will play a critical role in developing leaders, and resources, and it will serve as an epicenter for discussing issues critical to the global Black community. Dr. Elsie Scott, a past president of NCOBPS, and immediate past president and chief executive officer of the Congressional Black Caucus Foundation, was named founding director of the Dr. Ronald W. Walters Center, October 2, 2012.

Earlier this year, the book, *What Has This Got to Do with the Liberation of Black People: The Impact and Influence of Ronald Walters on Black Politics, Thought and Leadership*, a collection of papers on Ron's work, edited by Ron's former student, and long-time friend and collaborator, Robert Smith, was published as a tribute to Ron.

Here at the NPSR, we join those who continue to document the significance of Dr. Walters and his work, by offering in memoriam, an essay by William Strickland, who knew Ron as a friend and colleague in both the political and academic worlds. The title of Professor Strickland's essay is "Ron Walters: Black People's Strategist against the Politics of Post-Modern Racism in America."

Ron Walters: Black People's Strategist against the Politics of Post-Modern Racism in America

William Strickland
University of Massachusetts

(Writing this essay about Ron Walters has been one of my most daunting challenges . . . ever. I have written draft after draft, and then discarded each, one after the other, because none, to my satisfaction, captured Ron's specialness as a friend and confidant, nor his unique role as a steadfast, but scrupulously non-ostentatious activist, political strategist, and tireless advocate for the race. But the greatest challenge has been how to communicate to others my growing realization that Ron's story is also the story of our generation—and the story, writ small, of Black political struggle in America in the post-war world.)

Part One: The Myth of American Democracy

(To properly appreciate Ron's contribution, it is necessary to try, as best one can, to explain the political opposition that Black folk have faced historically, and the matura-tion of that opposition into the specific racial system that Ron strategized against for the past half-century.)

First of all, stripped of its historical cosmetics, the concept of American "democracy" does not withstand serious scrutiny. In fact, the concept of American exceptionalism is equally fanciful since America is simply one of a number of White settler states such as the former French Algeria, colonial Rhodesia, apartheid South Africa, Canada, huge swaths of South America, and other regions where indigenous people were enslaved, exterminated, and otherwise dominated so that White settlers could build a new "modern" society in their own (White) image.[1]

The success of this historical propaganda has led to an American phenomenon that I call the Candide syndrome, i.e., that most Americans, like Pangloss in Voltaire's *Candide*, believe that America is "the best of all possible worlds."

Black people and Native Americans, of course, given our experience in the country, do not subscribe to the alabaster myths and have struggled for centuries against the dispossession of our lands, the exploitation of our lives and labor, and the denial of our humanity.

Struggle is Black people's heritage in America: our struggle against slavery, our struggle against the serial betrayals of the Civil War and Reconstruction, our struggle against lynching and Jim Crow laws, our struggle against segregation and discrimination, our struggle for the right to vote, our struggle for freedom and equality, and our struggle just to be somebody in a land that has defined us as nobody. That is what "a nigger" is—a nobody.

But given the Candide syndrome, our struggle has always been solitary and uphill because the indoctrinated belief that America is "the best of all possible worlds" leads to a particular kind of political, intellectual, and theoretical denial. Since what is the need for a theory of change in America, "the best of all possible worlds"? And that is where Ron came in. Because Ron's life was a life dedicated, in theory and in practice, to deciphering—and combatting—the role of political racism in modern America.

Part Two: Enter the Modern Racist Counter-Revolution

(Racism has always been America's political lifeblood, the chief resource in empowering one political party or the other throughout American history. For most of Black history, because we have largely been a southern people, that party has been the Democratic Party, the party of the slave owners, the party of the assassins of Reconstruction, the party that built the Jim Crow society in the South and parented the southern Dixiecrats who defended segregation and lynching. But since 1968, the Republican Party has gained political advantage via its coded—and not-so-coded—racial policies and racial appeals. It has legitimized its right-wing perspective in the media and in mainstream political discourse. It has packed the courts and—with Democratic Party cooperation—championed unprecedented economic inequality in the nation, successfully transforming America's quasi-democratic state into an omnipotent corporate oligarchy.)[2]

One needs to recount this right-wing history because it is the history through which Ron lived, and is, I believe, fundamental to understanding his politics and world-view. Recounting it is also necessary because the absence of struggle in today's Black America is at odds with most of Ron's life and represents an historical discontinuity that thwarted many Black efforts at social change.

Unfortunately, the knowledge of our historical struggle is now missing in the lives of too many Black people born after the struggle's decline. This lacuna is in contrast with Ron's generation whose members had not lived through the Great Depression, but had learned of it from their parents and grandparents. They did know about Hitler and the Nazis, however, and they had *Jet* magazine, Black newspapers, and Black radio stations to tell them about the repetitive lynchings. Consequently, many of these young Blacks, in one venue or another, identified with the freedom struggle and took up political arms themselves.

I think that the knowledge of the politically possible, and the learned lessons of Black agency, sustained Ron throughout his life, and repeatedly fired his imagination on what could, or should, be done to further the cause of the race. But the politics of White supremacy, temporarily put back on its heels by the movement, came roaring back in the presidential election year of 1968 when all three candidates, Hubert Humphrey, Richard Nixon, and Alabama Governor George Wallace, demanded a return to "Law and Order" because something had to be done about the "Black savages" threatening to destroy their beloved nation. Indeed, in New York City, one group of Whites founded an organization called SPONGE, the Society for the Prevention of Negroes Getting Everything.

Nixon won the election narrowly over Humphrey by half a million votes: 31,785,000 to Humphrey's 31,275,000. Or 43.4 percent to 42.7 percent. George Wallace, repeating his 1964 pro-segregation appeal to the northern White working class, garnered ten million votes. Many of these votes came from outside the South, from states like Ohio, Indiana, and Wisconsin. But the significance of the election lay in the states won.

Republican Nixon won thirty-two states, including five southern states. Independent candidate, George Wallace, also won five southern states, and Democrat Hubert Humphrey won thirteen states and the District of Columbia. But Humphrey won only one southern state, Texas, probably due to Lyndon B. Johnson's (LBJ) influence. Few recognized at the time what a landmark Republican victory 1968 was and that it represented the success of the Republican "southern strategy" which had been agreed to in 1955 and which they called "Operation Dixie."[3]

That strategy was simply to compete with the southern Dixiecrats for the South's presidential vote by appealing to patriotism, militarism, homophobia, anti-feminism and, ever so slyly, racism. And why was the southern vote so important? Because of a little explained, or little understood, political procedure embedded in the U.S. Constitution in 1787 called the Electoral College which, then and now, really determines who will be the President of the United States.

Where do these electoral college votes come from? They represent the total number of senators and members of Congress in any presidential election year. So with two senators allotted to each of the fifty states and presently 435 members of Congress, the total electoral vote is 535. To become president, therefore, one need win only a majority of those 535 votes, or in present-day America, approximately 270 votes.

The Republican goal was to win the eleven states of the Old Confederacy because those southern states represent 161 electoral votes or 60 percent of the number needed to win the presidency. Thus, going back to the 1968 election, though Hubert Humphrey received almost as many popular votes as Richard Nixon, Nixon won 100 more electoral votes, 301 to 191. And with that advantage, Nixon won nineteen more states than the former vice-president. And there was another highly significant Republican coup rarely, if ever, discussed in the American press, and fearfully avoided by the Democratic Party: Nixon also won a majority of the White vote in 1968. More devastatingly, no Democratic Party candidate has won a majority of the White presidential vote since that time (including Barack Obama). To put the matter as plainly as possible, *no Democratic presidential candidate has won a majority of the White presidential vote in America since Lyndon Johnson in 1964*. And the success of the Republican appeal to the South was evident even then, since Lyndon lost five southern states to Barry Goldwater.

So playing racial politics relentlessly, the Republican Party for the past half-century has become the party of the White majority. This is the unacknowledged racial system that Ron Walters sought to combat at the National Black Political Convention held in Gary, Indiana, in 1972, the next presidential election year.

Part Three: The Gary Convention and Ron Walters' Strategic Black Politics

"There is no way to get to there but from here."—Karl Marx

The challenge for Ron—and everyone else at the National Black Political Convention— was how to cope with a political system that had, for all intents and purposes, turned its back on Black people. Nixon, for example, had won the election by opposing busing to facilitate school desegregation and by embracing South Carolina Senator Strom Thurmond, the former Klansman and 1948 Dixiecrat presidential candidate, who, seeing the way the racial wind was blowing, had left the Democratic Party and become a Republican.

Once in office, Nixon had sent a clear message of racial disdain in 1970 when he refused to meet with the nine Black members of the newly formed Congressional Black Caucus (the CBC), who wanted to "discuss his administration's policies vis-à-vis Blacks in the nation as a whole."[4]

That same year, Nixon made government indifference to the interests of Blacks official by asserting his administration's new policy of "benign neglect." He did so on the advice of his Counselor on Urban Affairs, Daniel Patrick Moynihan, an ostensible Democrat, who had worked for both the Kennedy and Johnson administrations before joining Nixon's White House staff in 1968.

As a Democrat, Moynihan had earlier published a Labor Department study on the Black family whose critics attacked it "as blaming the victim." (It is revealing that while 50 percent of White marriages during those years were ending in divorce, there was no similar criticism of White family structure.)

But Moynihan's advice was neither neutral nor blandly academic. Instead, in a private communiqué to Nixon, he had written:

> [S]ocial alienation among the black lower classes is matched, and probably enhanced, by a virulent form of anti-white feeling among portions of the large and prospering black middle class. It would be difficult to overestimate the degree to which young, well-educated blacks detest white America.[5]

Taking to heart Moynihan's analysis of the looming conflict between the races, Nixon hurriedly kept his campaign promise to reverse the decisions of the alleged civil rights leaning Justices of the Warren Supreme Court and appointed four new, right-leaning Justices, including the new Chief Justice, Warren Burger. Democrats failed to seriously oppose any of these appointments, carefully avoiding identifying themselves with potentially contentious racial issues. (They did, however, offer bipartisan support to what was now Nixon's war in Vietnam.)

Thus, evaluating the anti-Black policies of Nixon's first term, and scornful of a Democratic Party unwilling to join the fight against right-wing racism, 8,000 Black delegates came to the Gary Convention and stressed the need for independent Black politics. Its National Black Agenda insisted that if real change were to come to America, Black people must assume responsibility for making it, i.e.:

> We come to Gary in an hour of great crisis and tremendous promise for Black America. While the white nation hovers on the brink of chaos, while its politicians offer no hope of real change, we stand on the edge of history and are faced with an amazing and frightening choice: We may choose in 1972 to slip back into the decadent white politics of American life, or we may press forward, moving relentlessly from Gary to the creation of our own Black life.[6]

Regrettably, that hoped for, called for, racial unity did not materialize because too many Black delegates left Gary and went their own individual ways. The folly of that subservient course was amply demonstrated by the results of the 1972 election which Richard Nixon won overwhelmingly.

Nixon won forty-nine of the fifty states, including all the states of the Old Confederacy. George McGovern won Massachusetts and the District of Columbia. (Often referred to in those days because of the majority Black population as "Chocolate City!") George Wallace who had planned to run, and who might have been an important rival for the southern vote, had to withdraw from the campaign after he was shot in an assassination attempt in May.

But Ron left Gary buoyed by the experience. He felt that Gary, together with the thousands who later showed up in May in Washington, D.C., for African Liberation Day, signaled the beginning of a new Black political movement.

He affirmed this viewpoint in an article entitled, "The New Black Political Culture" that he wrote in October for Hoyt Fuller's magazine, *The Black World*:

> Every now and then events of such magnitude occur that *one needs to reach beyond the formalistic jargon of one's own training and tell the truth as he sees it*. . . . Now is the time for such truth-telling for there is a movement being born which will no doubt shape the politics of black people now and in the foreseeable future. . . . And here I refer to the concern for electoral politics at the National Black Political Convention in Gary, Indiana, and the thrust for African liberation in Washington, D.C.[7] (Emphasis mine.)

Ron then went on to indicate the direction that he believed the movement should take "to change *from Civil Rights to Black self-determination through electoral politics and African liberation*."[8] (Emphasis mine.)

Thus was born the political Ron Walters we came to know, admire, and depend upon, to penetrate America's superficial, ahistorical, and racially driven politics. He became our foremost strategist and theoretician on how to utilize an electoral political system designed not to advance but subvert our political fortunes. So Ron straddled two worlds. On the one hand, he was the consummate political idealist, committed to Black liberation and Black equality in an unequal world, on the other, he was the pragmatic idealist who realized that "*elections are not revolutionary instruments of change*."[9] Yet he counseled in 1975, on the eve of the 1976 presidential race, that:

> We [Black people] . . . are involved in a process of electing an administration which, *if it makes any changes at all, . . . will, at best be incremental*. This is not to say, however, that the activity is not worth the effort . . . [for]. *It is the only game being played of substance which relates to the problem of national leadership, and the problems of the black community can be attacked at no other level*.[10] (Emphasis mine.)

His advice then was that even though the deck was stacked against us, we still must play the game.

At the same time, Ron had no illusions about the vulnerability of Black elected officials, or BEOs, as he called them, who were embedded within a White power structure and who might pursue "a strategy of personal gain tied to their personal loyalties to white politicians, even at the sacrifice of the advancement of the total Black community."[11] Nevertheless, he argued that Blacks did have the potential power to leverage White politics on behalf of Black interests if the White votes were significantly divided and a united Black vote were mobilized in an independent racial vehicle such as a Black political party.

But while Ron was strategizing for us, the Democratic Party was given a gift from the gods: Richard Nixon was forced to resign the presidency in 1974 because of the Watergate scandal[12] and the presidency then passed on to his vice-president, former Congressman, Gerald Ford of Michigan.

Heartened by this development, the Democrats mounted their own "southern strategy" and chose Governor Jimmy Carter of Georgia as their presidential candidate.

Carter ran on the platform of "restoring faith in government" (after Watergate), and stressed his southern identity to counter the inroads that the Republicans had made in the South. This strategy seemed to pay off because Carter won all the southern states, except Virginia, and defeated Ford by slightly more than a million and a half votes.

But the race was much closer than the vote differential suggests because the states that Carter won were crucial. Indeed Ford actually won more states, 27 to 23. But Carter won the electoral vote, 297 to 240—due to the winning margin he gained in seven states worth 117 electoral votes where the Black vote was critical.

This balance of power performance was enough to catch Carter and the Democratic Party's eye and motivate them to, at least superficially, reward the Black electorate.

Accordingly, Carter appointed Blacks to his Cabinet and Andrew Young to the United Nations. These moves confirmed Ron's prediction of "incremental" rather than fundamental change. But, as he had warned, in the absence of an independent political organization of their own, Blacks were simply the recipients of whatever political gifts the Democratic Party and White House deigned to bestow upon us. This led Ron to now consider what kind of strategy might best overcome this servile and dependent relationship.

Part Four: Ron Walters and the Post-Movement Subversion of Black Politics

Political racism changes with the times—according to its needs, and in response to domestic or foreign pressures. But positive racial change is never permanent, never fixed.

The Cold War, for example, forced a superficial and public relations alteration in America's racial posture since rampant, unchecked, and public racism tended to impugn America's claim to be "the land of the free." Thus in 1954, for foreign policy's sake, Eisenhower's Attorney General, Herbert Brownell, joined with the National Association for the Advancement of Colored People (NAACP) in arguing against school segregation before the Supreme Court. Brownell urged the Justices to be mindful of America's image abroad and asked that "the separate but equal doctrine be stricken down . . . [because] . . . it furnishes grist for the communist propaganda mills, and it raises doubt, even among friendly nations, as to the intensity of our devotion to the democratic faith."[13] The mass movement had not yet erupted when Brownell made his plea. But shortly thereafter, working together with House Majority Leader, Lyndon Johnson, the Eisenhower administration took the small but hesitant step to pass the Civil Rights Acts of 1957 and 1960—the year when John Fitzgerald Kennedy (JFK) was elected president and Black students launched the sit-in movement in the South. Ready or not, thereafter, Kennedy was thrust headlong into a student-led movement that would escalate from sit-ins to voter registration in some of the most backward regions of the South.

Kennedy did his best to try to temper the students, but they would not be tempered. Then he was assassinated in November of 1963, and Lyndon Johnson, his vice-president, became President of the United States.

Johnson, to his credit, on the home front, as opposed to his machinations in Vietnam, initiated more government entitlement programs specifically relevant to Blacks than any president, before or since. He called for an inclusive "Great Society" and made "War on Poverty." He established Volunteers in Service to America (VISTA), the Job Corps, the

Economic Opportunity Act, the Head Start Program for Children, etc. For the first time since Reconstruction, the American government was, for a little while, a semi-ally of Black people. But then came Nixon's "benign neglect" retreat and, after Nixon, Reagan's full-scale governmental assault.

Reagan kicked off his 1980 campaign against Jimmy Carter by sending the most glaring and obvious racist signal imaginable. He traveled to the little backwoods town of Philadelphia, Mississippi, where the three civil rights workers, Andy Goodman, Michael Schwerner, and James Chaney had been murdered in 1964. He went there, he claimed, to show his support for States Rights. But his message was clear to all—especially to the Ku Klux Klan who quickly endorsed him. Reagan turned down their endorsement, of course. But the message had been sent: The segregationist train was leaving the station and Blacks would not be allowed on board. It was no surprise then that in the election itself, Reagan won all the old Confederate states—except Carter's home state of Georgia.

Once in office, Reagan waged total underhanded war against Black people. He filed *amicus curiae* briefs on behalf of segregated schools and fought the extension of the civil rights laws. He undermined the Civil Rights Commission and packed the federal courts with his ideological allies. He opposed affirmative action relentlessly and victimized Black children by cutting back pre-natal care. He virtually eliminated housing subsidies and tried to shut down any programs offered by the Small Business Administration that might help Black entrepreneurs. And he pioneered Reaganomics, the ridiculous doctrine of "trickle-down" economics that alleged that spending cuts of social programs and tax cuts for the rich would somehow benefit the taxpayers whose money was being handed to the corporations—and to what is now the One Percent.

Thus in his two terms in office, Reagan plunged the federal government into deeper debt—three trillion dollars!—than had previously been incurred in the whole history of the United States. And yet he is still portrayed as someone who is to be looked up to in American politics. The Right had, at one point, even promoted a campaign to put Reagan on Mt. Rushmore with Washington, Lincoln, Jefferson, and Teddy Roosevelt. And Obama, for some unknown and uninformed reason, has cited Reagan as a worthy role model.

This is the bleak picture that Ron Walters encountered after leaving Gary and returning to Washington, D.C., and Howard University, where he had received a Ford Foundation grant in 1971 to develop a graduate program in political science. He plunged right in, of course, and despite the egocentric and corruption-disposed nature of D.C. politics, Ron set out to achieve his twin political goals of wedding—and advancing—the Black struggle in America to the liberation struggle in Africa.

Part Five: Fighting Apartheid Abroad and Racist "Tricknology" at Home

As a scholar required to teach as well as administer and secure funding for a graduate program in political science that had to be created from scratch, Ron was swamped with myriad duties that impeded his desired activism.[14] However, he solved the problem of gaining access to electoral politics, and influencing it as best he could, by becoming a key aide to Congressman Charles Diggs of Michigan, the first Chairman of the Congressional Black Caucus, and its leading expert on African affairs. Bringing apartheid to an end was a mutual goal shared by Ron and the CBC, so in 1977 when Ron co-founded TransAfrica, the Black organization that analyzed events in Africa and the Caribbean and lobbied on their behalf, it was a natural kinship for the two groups to spearhead the Free South Africa movement which, later, sparked thousands of protests against apartheid in 1985. This deluge of demonstrations was inspired by the 1984 arrests of Randall Robinson, the Executive Director of TransAfrica; D.C. Congressman and former aide to Martin Luther King, Jr., Walter Fauntroy; and Civil Rights Commissioner, Mary Berry, who all sat in at the Washington office of the Ambassador of South Africa.

In 1986, to further bolster the Free South Africa forces, the CBC authored the Comprehensive Anti-Apartheid Act, to prevent U.S. loans to, and investments in, South Africa. That proposed legislation pressured Reagan into signing a less stringent executive order to prevent the Act from becoming a more binding law. However, the struggle against apartheid was successfully concluded in 1994 when Nelson Mandela was elected President of South Africa. (Ron was a member of the U.S. delegation that monitored that triumphal election.)

Unfortunately, that victory abroad was not matched by similar victories at home because the CBC's never-ending struggle with the Reagan administration over extending the Voting Rights Act and even making Martin Luther King, Jr.'s birthday a national holiday, signified the adamant White political resistance to the restructuring of America into an equal rights nation. Indeed, almost as soon as the Voting Rights Act was passed in 1965, the subsequent upsurge in the election of Black elected officials motivated the agents of White supremacy to devise new strategies and tactics to negate this progress.

The most striking—and immediate—evidence of the White-imposed sunset on the new political day occurred in 1967 when Dick Hatcher was elected mayor of Gary, Indiana; and Carl Stokes was elected mayor of Cleveland, Ohio. As illustration of the systematic malevolence, I want to quote an excerpt from Carl Stokes' book, *Promises of Power*, that vividly describes the multifaceted and nefarious opposition that awaited practically all Black elected officials who got their feet on the first rung of the ladder of Black political power:

> Practices that had been going on for years were suddenly being investigated during my administration. . . . Things that were not crimes were made to seem like crimes to discredit my administration.
>
> Accordingly, I was investigated by everyone from Cleveland's lowliest Polish housewife to the highest agencies of the U.S. government, my own police department, all of the Cleveland area newspapers, the strike force set up to fight organized crime, the Justice Department, the Internal Revenue Service were all in Cleveland and anywhere I'd ever been, investigating me because of rumors, allegations, and accusations. . . . Efforts to physically assassinate me were successfully warded off, but there was no way to ward off the systematic and determined campaign to assassinate me with rumor, conjecture, speculation, insinuation, and indirect charges that I had no defense against.[15]

Carl Stokes faced not only physical assassination but also the most formidable array of racial opponents conceivable. He was fair game for all. Though he is not specific about the time period of the federal investigations, if they occurred in the first years of his administration, they were as likely to have been authorized by a Democratic as by a Republican administration.

The fate awaiting Black elected officials was outright hostility from Republicans, and lukewarm or standoffish behavior from "fellow" Democrats who feared that "what many whites viewed as 'Black issues'—federal efforts in regard to residential segregation, affirmative action, social programs for the poor, and criminal justice reform—were alienating many white voters . . . [so] . . . white Democratic leaders gradually backed off on strongly supporting important civil rights goals, just as Republicans had done earlier."[16]

Politically speaking, we were orphans in the land. And then, along came Jesse.

Emboldened by Harold Washington's mayoral victory in Chicago in 1983 despite the fact that 80 percent of White Democrats voted for Harold's Republican opponent, Bernard Epton—Jesse announced his candidacy for president later that year. Naturally he reached out for Ron who had, serendipitously, given two talks on "The Black Presidential Candidacy" in April and May, before the National Conference of Black Political Scientists and the Joint Center for Political Studies.

Jesse had marked well the lessons of Harold's successful race: that 150,000 Blacks were newly registered; that the total Black turnout was 73 percent versus 67 percent for Whites; that Blacks had voted for Harold practically 100 percent, and that Hispanics gave him 75 percent of their votes. Even Whites, who had voted for Harold at only 6 percent in the primary, doubled their support to 12 percent in the general election. It did not therefore take a rocket scientist to figure out that a coalition of Blacks, Browns, and Whites could win an electoral victory even where registered Whites were a majority which, in the case of Chicago, was 53 percent.[17] And if it could be done in Chicago, why could it not be done in the nation as a whole? Thus was born Jesse Jackson's Rainbow Coalition with its special appeal to Blacks:

> We were not brought from Africa to be white people's slaves. But perhaps we were sent here by God to save the nation. . . . Our day has come. From slave ship to championship . . . from the outhouse to the courthouse to the White House, we will march on.[18]

Ron joined Jesse's campaign as one of his top aides in 1984 and 1988 and wrote a book, *Black Presidential Politics in America: A Strategic Approach* (1988), based on Jesse's first campaign. In the book he described his own experience as a member of the exploratory committee that originally researched the feasibility of Jesse's run and his subsequent role as Jesse's Deputy Campaign Manager for Issues and Political Strategy.

In retrospect, he concluded that what he called "the essential strategy" of a substantial group of Black elected officials who had hoped to foment great change by participating in presidential politics had yielded very few concrete gains, and that this "dependent strategy" had to be replaced by an independent autonomous organization because, "the Democratic party coalition appears to be . . . attempting to readjust its liberal social legacy of the New Deal to the more conservative political and economic trends of the 1980s and 1990s." Ron's prediction was accurate. Once again, the Democratic Party's determination to skirt all relevant issues and copycat the Republicans' right-wing perspective produced the same result in 1984 as it had in 1972.

Walter Mondale, the 1984 Democratic presidential candidate and Jimmy Carter's former vice-president—like McGovern—in 1972—won one state, his home state of Minnesota, and the District of Columbia. Reagan won the other forty-nine states. Even purloining Jesse's idea of putting a female on the ticket as a vice-presidential nominee availed Mondale nothing—which was the same prize won by the Black Democrats who supported Mondale because they did not believe most White Americans would vote for a Black presidential candidate. By 1988, however, the Black Democrats had come around and backed Jesse. Even Andy Young, who had also declined to support Jesse at the 1984 Democratic Convention in San Francisco, excoriated Mondale's advisors as "smart-ass white boys [sic] who think they know it all," and came over to the Rainbow in 1988.

It is difficult not to believe that had the Democrats nominated Jesse in 1984, that he could hardly have done worse than Mondale. But despite the fact that Jesse was the only real critic of Reagan and Reaganism, the Democrats failed even to consider Jesse for the vice-presidential slot in 1988. Instead, Massachusetts Governor, Michael Dukakis, selected Lloyd Bentsen of Texas. Still, Jesse remained party loyal, registering tens of thousands of Blacks to aid the Democratic ticket. He failed, however, to follow Ron's theory of "independent leverage to accomplish the organization and direction of Black political resources." Thus a golden opportunity was lost because, after his 1984 campaign, 53 percent of Blacks said that they were prepared to follow Jesse into an independent Black political whatever. History had knocked. But neither Jesse nor Black elected officials chose to answer.

The Democratic Party's lack of nerve, and its failure to confront the politics of racism, next lost them the 1988 election when George Bush, Reagan's vice-president, accused Dukakis of being soft on crime because he had granted a prison furlough to Black inmate, Willie Horton, who fled the program and raped a White woman. And in case the racist message was not entirely clear, Bush linked Dukakis to Jesse by telling the White electorate that a vote for Dukakis would be equivalent to putting Jesse in the White House. Dukakis then, unforgivably, tried to counter the accusation of being so decidedly pro-Black by going to Philadelphia, Mississippi—just as Reagan had done in 1980. But that little racist flim-flam did not fool the real White supremacists. Dukakis won no southern state. Though, like his party predecessors, he did win the District of Columbia.

Before Jesse, for a decade and a half, since 1968, there had been no Black mass movement in America. Then Jesse mobilized the people once again and tempted them with the scent of political power and social change. But it all came to an end in 1988, leaving us without a leader—or a movement—to confront the new racism that called itself conservatism. (In modern times, racists are called "social conservatives" while Wall Street and corporate lackeys who want all tax money to go to the military and multinational corporations are called "fiscal conservatives.")[19]

Indeed, given the wasteland of political desertedness, things got so desperate that some Black people invented leadership where none existed, portraying Bill Clinton as the "black people's president."[20] Ron, of course, told it like it was in another book, *White Nationalism/ Black Interests: Conservative Public Policy and the Black Community* (2003):

> Today, it is often unfashionable to be openly racist in many quarters, and the fact that racists have adopted the convenient cloak of conservatism under which to hide is a matter which makes the two often difficult to separate. The result is that White nationalism has permeated the highest political institutions in the country and . . . affects the formation of public policy in important ways. The linkage between white racism and white nationalism is that those whites may be defined into the nationalist movement who have . . . utilized the political system to enact a new regime of social control over Blacks and other people of color as a subtext of their policy "reform." Politics and policy are [thus] the new instruments of social [repression], although there is still open racism practiced both officially and unofficially.

But the worse was yet to come. After Clinton came the Bush-Cheney Republicans so steeped in anti-Black sentiment that there was no racial practice too foul for them to employ. One classic example was "how Republican and other conservative political operatives ... arranged to have Democratic Party phone banks jammed so they could not reach voters and used actors with fake 'ghetto' or Spanish accents to make calls supposedly for Democratic candidates, to white voters whom the Republicans felt might be scared off by such accents."[21]

The political situation seemed so unpromising to Ron that he looked to South Africa's Truth and Reconciliation Commission as one possible way of rectifying racial inequality in America. So in 2008, as Bush was nearing his last year in office, Ron penned *The Price of Racial Reconciliation* in which he sought to expose the right-wing rejection of America's racist reality as the falsehood that it was:

> This book is dedicated to deconstructing the fiction that slavery and post-slavery racism are unrelated to the current socio-economic status of Blacks in America, and that the past history of Black subordination is, or ever has been, without consequences to Blacks in the present, or to American society in general. It reemphasizes the demand for reparations by discussing issues that were confronted in the paradigm of racial reconciliation in South Africa, which led to the development of the Truth and Reconciliation Commission there.[22]

Ron stayed the course. From Gary in 1972 to Obama's election in 2008, he had lectured, taught, written, counseled, traveled abroad, and coped. He had seen his long-cherished hope and long-argued for strategy of a successful Black presidential campaign come to life in Obama's energizing of a new de facto Rainbow Coalition. But Ron was not completely swept off his feet. He still asked the right questions and still judged Obama through the lens of Black political history and the unmet expectations that came solely from relying on the politics of hope. Thus, during the course of Obama's campaign in July of 2008 he articulated his uneasiness:

> [W]hat concerns me is that we are involved in a great celebration without checking the guidepost that determines whether or not there will be sufficient returns to our community from a black president in the White House. The irony is that Obama is likely to win, we will have to accept him, but under circumstances where he is essentially a white candidate. So we should "bottom line our public policy requirements now as every other community is doing."

A year later, in May, 2009, he sent me an email that he was "working on a book on Obama featuring my op-ed pieces." That was my man Ron. Till the end, seeking truth over illusion.

Someone once said that when someone dies a library closes. In Ron's case, we have lost not merely a library, but a whole university. So take care, baby. Love you.

Notes

1. Bill Strickland, "Things Fall Apart: Black Struggle in Imperial America and the Need for an Adequate Theory of Emancipation for the 21st Century," *The Black Scholar* 34, no. 3 (Fall 2004): 2.
2. Although the Republican Party is the favorite of corporations and Wall Street, it was the Clinton administration's Secretary of the Treasury, Robert Rubin, and his assistant, Larry Summers, who joined with Republicans in 1999 to torpedo the 1933 Glass-Steagall Act passed during the Depression to regulate the banks. Obama later appointed Summers his chief economic advisor.
3. Philip A. Klinkner and Rogers M. Smith, *The Unsteady March: The Rise and Decline of Racial Equality in America* (Chicago: University of Chicago Press, 1999), 261–62.
4. Robert H. Brisbane, *Racial Revolution in the United States, 1954–1970.* (Valley Forge: Judson Press, 1974), 262.

5. Lucius J. Barker and Jesse J. McCorry, Jr., *Black Americans and the Political System* (Cambridge: Winthrop Publishers, 1976), 334.
6. *Black World* 21, no. 12 (October 1972): 27.
7. *The Black World*, 5.
8. Ibid., 4.
9. Ronald Walters, "Strategy for 1976: A Black Political Party," *The Black Scholar* 7, no. 2 (October 1975): 9.
10. Ibid., 8–9.
11. Ibid., 12.
12. In June of 1972, five agents of CREEP, the Committee to Re-elect the President, were arrested for breaking into the Democratic Party's national office in the Watergate hotel. It turned out that this was only one of several "dirty tricks" ordered by the White House that then tried to cover up its role. But impeachment proceedings in July of 1974 prompted Nixon to resign in August. However, Ford pardoned him in September "for all the offenses which he has committed . . . or may have committed against the United States."
13. Bill Strickland, "The Road Since Brown: The Americanization of the Race," *The Black Scholar* 11, no. 1 (September–October 1979): 3.
14. "Tricknology" was Malcolm X's concept of the methods of duplicity employed by America to equal its hypocrisy in race relations and deceive, i.e., "trick" the Blacks whom it was subjugating.
15. Mary R. Warner, *The Dilemma of Black Politics: A Report on the Harassment of Black Elected Officials* (Sacramento: M.R. Warner, 1977), 146–47.
16. Joe Feagin, *White Party, White Government* (New York: Routledge, 2012), 118.
17. Steven F. Lawson, *Running for Freedom: Civil Rights and Black Politics in America since 1941* (Philadelphia: Temple University Press, 1991).
18. Ibid., 226.
19. Robert Smith, *Conservatism and Racism, and Why in America They Are the Same* (Albany: State University of New York Press, 2010).
20. DeWayne Wickham, *Bill Clinton and Black America* (New York: Ballantine Books, 2002).
21. Feagin, 135.
22. Ronald W. Walters, *The Price of Racial Reconciliation* (Ann Arbor: University of Michigan Press, 2008).

The National Political Science Review (NPSR)

Invitation to the Scholarly Community

The editors of *The National Political Science Review* (NPSR) invite submissions from the scholarly community for review and possible publication.

The NPSR is a refereed journal of the National Conference of Black Political Scientists. Its editions appear annually and comprise the highest quality scholarship related to the experiences of African Americans in the American political community as well as in the wider reach of the African diaspora in the Western Hemisphere. It also focuses on the international links between African Americans and the larger community of nations, particularly with Africa.

Among the more common areas of research which the NPSR considers for publication are those typically associated with political behavior and attitudes, the performance of political institutions, the efficacy of public policy, interest groups and social movements, inter-ethnic coalition building, and theoretical reflections which offer insights on the minority political experience. Based on recent interest the NPSR also considers work on the role of culture in politics.

Manuscripts should be submitted in the following format. Submissions should follow the style conventions of the *American Political Science Review* (APSR). Two copies of the submissions should be conveyed electronically to the editors at the email addresses listed below. One copy of the submission should include the author's or authors' information comprising of the name that will appear in the published version along with the author's/authors' institutional affiliation and email addresses. The other copy should delete the author's/authors' information from the title page. Please indicate the lead author and email address in cases of multiple authors. Manuscripts should not carry footnotes at the bottom of the page. They should not exceed thirty (30) typewritten pages, double spaced, inclusive of notes and references, and should be prepared and sent to the editors in Microsoft Word format.

Manuscripts are reviewed on a rolling basis. However, submissions should be received no later than July 1 of the current year to be considered for publication in a forthcoming issue.

Further queries about the NPSR as well as submissions may be addressed (email only) to the editors at:

Michael Mitchell
Co-Editor of the NPSR
School of Politics and Global Studies
Arizona State University
email: michael.mitchell@asu.edu

David Covin
Co-Editor of the NPSR
Government Department (Emeritus)
California State University-Sacramento
email: covindl@csus.edu